50 Low-Carb Thai Salad Recipes for Home

By: Kelly Johnson

Table of Contents

- Thai Beef Salad with Spicy Lime Dressing
- Low-carb Thai Chicken Satay Salad
- Thai Shrimp and Avocado Salad
- Thai-style Spicy Tofu Salad
- Low-carb Thai Pork Larb Salad
- Thai Eggplant Salad with Chili Dressing
- Thai Green Papaya Salad with Shrimp
- Low-carb Thai Turkey Larb Salad
- Thai-style Grilled Fish Salad
- Thai Cucumber Salad with Peanut Dressing
- Low-carb Thai Crab Salad with Lemongrass
- Thai-style Zucchini Noodle Salad
- Low-carb Thai Beef Larb Lettuce Wraps
- Thai-style Cauliflower Rice Salad with Chicken
- Low-carb Thai Chicken Larb Lettuce Cups
- Thai-inspired Spicy Beef Salad with Mint
- Low-carb Thai Tofu Larb Lettuce Wraps
- Thai-style Grilled Chicken and Vegetable Salad
- Low-carb Thai Pork Larb Lettuce Wraps
- Thai-inspired Cabbage Salad with Spicy Dressing
- Low-carb Thai Shrimp Larb Lettuce Cups
- Thai-style Grilled Eggplant Salad with Sesame Dressing
- Low-carb Thai Turkey Larb Lettuce Wraps
- Thai-inspired Broccoli Salad with Peanut Dressing
- Low-carb Thai Beef Salad with Cucumber Ribbons
- Thai-style Seared Tuna Salad with Spicy Dressing
- Low-carb Thai Chicken Larb Salad with Lettuce Wraps
- Thai-inspired Asparagus Salad with Chili Lime Dressing
- Low-carb Thai Spicy Pork Salad with Herbs
- Thai-style Grilled Mushroom Salad with Soy Ginger Dressing
- Low-carb Thai Shrimp Larb Salad with Mint
- Thai-inspired Radish Salad with Lime Dressing
- Low-carb Thai Chicken Satay Zoodle Salad
- Thai-style Spicy Beef Larb Lettuce Wraps
- Low-carb Thai Turkey Larb Salad with Cucumber

- Thai-inspired Brussels Sprouts Salad with Sesame Dressing
- Low-carb Thai Tofu Larb Salad with Lime
- Thai-style Grilled Salmon Salad with Coconut Dressing
- Low-carb Thai Pork Larb Salad with Cabbage
- Thai-inspired Green Bean Salad with Peanut Dressing
- Low-carb Thai Chicken Larb Salad with Bell Peppers
- Thai-style Spicy Beef Salad with Basil
- Low-carb Thai Shrimp Larb Salad with Cilantro
- Thai-inspired Cabbage Salad with Fish Sauce Dressing
- Low-carb Thai Turkey Larb Salad with Mint
- Thai-style Grilled Squid Salad with Lime Dressing
- Low-carb Thai Tofu Larb Salad with Lemongrass
- Thai-inspired Egg Salad with Chili Lime Dressing
- Low-carb Thai Beef Salad with Bean Sprouts
- Thai-style Spicy Pork Larb Lettuce Wraps

Thai Beef Salad with Spicy Lime Dressing

Ingredients:

- 1 lb (450g) beef steak (such as sirloin or flank), thinly sliced
- 4 cups mixed salad greens (such as lettuce, spinach, or arugula)
- 1 cucumber, thinly sliced
- 1 red onion, thinly sliced
- 1-2 tomatoes, sliced
- 1/4 cup fresh cilantro leaves, chopped
- 1/4 cup fresh mint leaves, chopped
- 1/4 cup roasted peanuts, chopped (optional)
- 2-3 cloves garlic, minced
- 2-3 Thai bird's eye chilies, minced (adjust to taste)
- 3 tablespoons fish sauce
- 3 tablespoons lime juice
- 2 tablespoons soy sauce
- 1 tablespoon brown sugar
- 1 tablespoon vegetable oil
- Salt and pepper to taste

Instructions:

1. Marinate the Beef: In a bowl, combine the sliced beef with minced garlic, minced Thai chilies, soy sauce, and vegetable oil. Let it marinate for at least 30 minutes, or up to 2 hours in the refrigerator.
2. Prepare the Dressing: In a small bowl, whisk together fish sauce, lime juice, and brown sugar until the sugar is dissolved. Taste and adjust the seasoning as needed. If you prefer it spicier, add more minced Thai chilies.
3. Cook the Beef: Heat a grill pan or skillet over medium-high heat. Cook the marinated beef slices for 2-3 minutes on each side, or until cooked to your desired doneness. Remove from heat and let it rest for a few minutes.
4. Assemble the Salad: In a large mixing bowl, combine the mixed salad greens, sliced cucumber, sliced red onion, sliced tomatoes, chopped cilantro, and chopped mint leaves.
5. Add the Beef and Dressing: Arrange the cooked beef slices on top of the salad. Drizzle the spicy lime dressing over the salad and beef.
6. Garnish and Serve: Sprinkle chopped roasted peanuts over the salad for extra crunch and flavor. Serve immediately and enjoy!

Feel free to customize the salad by adding other vegetables like bell peppers, carrots, or bean sprouts, and adjust the level of spiciness according to your preference. It's a versatile dish that's perfect for a light lunch or dinner. Enjoy!

Low-carb Thai Chicken Satay Salad

Ingredients:

For the Chicken Satay:

- 1 lb (450g) boneless, skinless chicken breasts or thighs, cut into thin strips
- 3 tablespoons coconut milk
- 2 tablespoons soy sauce or tamari (for gluten-free option)
- 1 tablespoon fish sauce
- 1 tablespoon lime juice
- 1 tablespoon curry powder
- 1 teaspoon turmeric powder
- 1 teaspoon garlic powder
- 1 teaspoon ginger powder
- 1 tablespoon olive oil or coconut oil for grilling

For the Salad:

- 4 cups mixed salad greens (such as lettuce, spinach, or kale)
- 1 cucumber, thinly sliced
- 1 red bell pepper, thinly sliced
- 1/4 cup chopped cilantro
- 1/4 cup chopped peanuts or almonds (optional)

For the Peanut Sauce:

- 1/4 cup creamy peanut butter (unsweetened)
- 2 tablespoons coconut milk
- 1 tablespoon soy sauce or tamari
- 1 tablespoon lime juice
- 1 teaspoon fish sauce
- 1 teaspoon sriracha sauce (adjust to taste)
- 1 teaspoon minced garlic
- Water (to adjust consistency)

Instructions:

1. Marinate the Chicken:

- In a bowl, combine coconut milk, soy sauce, fish sauce, lime juice, curry powder, turmeric powder, garlic powder, and ginger powder.
- Add the chicken strips to the marinade, ensuring they are evenly coated. Marinate for at least 30 minutes in the refrigerator.

2. Prepare the Peanut Sauce:
    - In a small saucepan over low heat, combine peanut butter, coconut milk, soy sauce, lime juice, fish sauce, sriracha sauce, and minced garlic.
    - Stir until the sauce is smooth and well combined. If the sauce is too thick, add water gradually until desired consistency is reached. Set aside.

3. Grill the Chicken:
    - Heat a grill pan or skillet over medium-high heat. Brush with olive oil or coconut oil.
    - Thread the marinated chicken strips onto skewers and grill for 3-4 minutes on each side, or until cooked through and slightly charred. Remove from heat and set aside.

4. Assemble the Salad:
    - In a large salad bowl, combine mixed greens, sliced cucumber, sliced red bell pepper, and chopped cilantro.

5. Add the Chicken:
    - Remove the chicken from skewers and place on top of the salad.

6. Serve:
    - Drizzle the peanut sauce over the salad or serve it on the side.
    - Optional: Garnish with chopped peanuts or almonds for extra crunch and flavor.

This low-carb Thai Chicken Satay Salad is packed with flavor and nutrients, making it a satisfying and healthy meal option. Enjoy!

Thai Shrimp and Avocado Salad

Ingredients:

For the Salad:

- 1 lb (450g) large shrimp, peeled and deveined
- 2 ripe avocados, diced
- 4 cups mixed salad greens (such as lettuce, spinach, or arugula)
- 1 cucumber, thinly sliced
- 1/2 red onion, thinly sliced
- 1/4 cup fresh cilantro leaves, chopped
- 1/4 cup fresh mint leaves, chopped
- 1/4 cup roasted peanuts, chopped (optional)
- Salt and pepper to taste

For the Dressing:

- 3 tablespoons lime juice
- 2 tablespoons fish sauce
- 1 tablespoon soy sauce
- 1 tablespoon honey or maple syrup
- 1 tablespoon sesame oil
- 1 teaspoon grated ginger
- 1 garlic clove, minced
- 1 Thai bird's eye chili, minced (optional, adjust to taste)

Instructions:

1. Prepare the Shrimp:
   - Season the shrimp with salt and pepper. You can also add a pinch of chili powder or paprika for extra flavor if desired.
   - Heat a skillet or grill pan over medium-high heat. Cook the shrimp for 2-3 minutes on each side until they turn pink and opaque. Remove from heat and set aside.
2. Prepare the Dressing:
   - In a small bowl, whisk together lime juice, fish sauce, soy sauce, honey or maple syrup, sesame oil, grated ginger, minced garlic, and minced Thai chili (if using). Adjust the seasoning to taste.

3. Assemble the Salad:
    - In a large mixing bowl, combine the mixed salad greens, diced avocado, sliced cucumber, sliced red onion, chopped cilantro, and chopped mint leaves.
    - Add the cooked shrimp to the salad.
4. Add the Dressing:
    - Drizzle the dressing over the salad and gently toss to coat everything evenly.
5. Garnish and Serve:
    - Sprinkle chopped roasted peanuts over the salad for extra texture and flavor, if desired.
    - Serve the Thai Shrimp and Avocado Salad immediately as a light and refreshing meal.

Feel free to customize the salad by adding other vegetables such as bell peppers or cherry tomatoes. Adjust the level of spiciness in the dressing according to your preference. Enjoy this delicious and healthy Thai-inspired salad!

Thai-style Spicy Tofu Salad

Ingredients:

For the Tofu:

- 1 block (about 14 oz or 400g) extra-firm tofu, pressed and cubed
- 2 tablespoons cornstarch
- 2 tablespoons soy sauce
- 1 tablespoon sesame oil
- 1 tablespoon vegetable oil for frying

For the Salad:

- 4 cups mixed salad greens (such as lettuce, spinach, or arugula)
- 1 red bell pepper, thinly sliced
- 1 cucumber, thinly sliced
- 1 carrot, julienned or thinly sliced
- 1/4 cup fresh cilantro leaves, chopped
- 1/4 cup fresh mint leaves, chopped
- 1/4 cup roasted peanuts, chopped (optional)

For the Dressing:

- 3 tablespoons lime juice
- 2 tablespoons fish sauce (or soy sauce for a vegetarian option)
- 1 tablespoon soy sauce
- 1 tablespoon honey or maple syrup
- 1 tablespoon sesame oil
- 1 teaspoon grated ginger
- 1 garlic clove, minced
- 1 Thai bird's eye chili, minced (adjust to taste)

Instructions:

1. Prepare the Tofu:
   - Press the tofu to remove excess water. Cut it into cubes and pat dry with paper towels.
   - In a bowl, toss the tofu cubes with cornstarch until evenly coated.

- In a separate small bowl, mix soy sauce and sesame oil. Drizzle this mixture over the tofu cubes and toss to coat.
2. Fry the Tofu:
   - Heat vegetable oil in a skillet over medium-high heat. Once hot, add the tofu cubes in a single layer.
   - Fry the tofu for 2-3 minutes on each side until golden and crispy. Remove from the skillet and place on a paper towel-lined plate to drain excess oil.
3. Prepare the Dressing:
   - In a small bowl, whisk together lime juice, fish sauce (or soy sauce), soy sauce, honey or maple syrup, sesame oil, grated ginger, minced garlic, and minced Thai chili (adjust to taste). Set aside.
4. Assemble the Salad:
   - In a large mixing bowl, combine the mixed salad greens, sliced red bell pepper, sliced cucumber, julienned carrot, chopped cilantro, and chopped mint leaves.
   - Add the crispy tofu cubes to the salad.
5. Add the Dressing:
   - Drizzle the dressing over the salad and gently toss to coat everything evenly.
6. Garnish and Serve:
   - Sprinkle chopped roasted peanuts over the salad for extra crunch and flavor, if desired.
   - Serve the Thai-style Spicy Tofu Salad immediately as a delicious and satisfying meal.

Feel free to customize the salad by adding other vegetables such as cherry tomatoes, bean sprouts, or shredded cabbage. Adjust the level of spiciness in the dressing according to your preference. Enjoy this flavorful and nutritious Thai-inspired salad!

Low-carb Thai Pork Larb Salad

Ingredients:

For the Pork Larb:

- 1 lb (450g) ground pork
- 2 tablespoons vegetable oil
- 3 shallots, finely chopped
- 3 cloves garlic, minced
- 1-2 Thai bird's eye chilies, finely chopped (adjust to taste)
- 2 tablespoons fish sauce
- 2 tablespoons lime juice
- 1 tablespoon soy sauce or tamari (for gluten-free option)
- 1 teaspoon erythritol or monk fruit sweetener (optional)
- 1/4 cup fresh cilantro leaves, chopped
- 1/4 cup fresh mint leaves, chopped
- 2 green onions, thinly sliced
- Salt and pepper to taste

For the Salad:

- 4 cups mixed salad greens (such as lettuce, spinach, or arugula)
- 1 cucumber, thinly sliced
- 1/2 cup cherry tomatoes, halved
- 1/4 cup chopped peanuts or almonds (optional)
- Lime wedges for serving

Instructions:

1. Cook the Pork Larb:
   - Heat vegetable oil in a skillet over medium-high heat. Add shallots, garlic, and Thai chilies. Sauté until fragrant, about 1-2 minutes.
   - Add the ground pork to the skillet, breaking it up with a spoon. Cook until the pork is browned and cooked through, about 5-7 minutes.
   - Stir in fish sauce, lime juice, soy sauce, and erythritol or monk fruit sweetener (if using). Cook for an additional 2-3 minutes.
   - Remove from heat and stir in chopped cilantro, chopped mint, and sliced green onions. Season with salt and pepper to taste.

2. Assemble the Salad:
   - In a large mixing bowl, combine the mixed salad greens, sliced cucumber, and halved cherry tomatoes.
   - Add the cooked pork larb to the salad and toss to combine.
3. Garnish and Serve:
   - Sprinkle chopped peanuts or almonds over the salad for extra crunch and flavor.
   - Serve the low-carb Thai Pork Larb Salad with lime wedges on the side for squeezing over the salad.

This low-carb Thai Pork Larb Salad is bursting with flavor and makes a satisfying meal on its own. Feel free to adjust the seasoning and spice level according to your preference. Enjoy!

Thai Eggplant Salad with Chili Dressing

Ingredients:

For the Salad:

- 2 medium-sized Asian eggplants or 1 large globe eggplant
- 2 tablespoons vegetable oil
- Salt, to taste
- 1/4 cup chopped fresh cilantro
- 2 tablespoons chopped green onions
- 1 tablespoon chopped roasted peanuts (optional, for garnish)

For the Chili Dressing:

- 2 tablespoons lime juice
- 1 tablespoon fish sauce
- 1 tablespoon soy sauce or tamari (for gluten-free option)
- 1 tablespoon honey or maple syrup
- 1-2 Thai bird's eye chilies, finely chopped (adjust to taste)
- 2 cloves garlic, minced

Instructions:

1. Prepare the Eggplants:
   - If using Asian eggplants, slice them into rounds. If using globe eggplant, dice them into bite-sized pieces.
   - Heat vegetable oil in a skillet over medium heat. Add the eggplant slices or cubes in a single layer. Cook until golden brown and tender, flipping halfway through. Sprinkle with salt while cooking. Remove from heat and set aside.
2. Make the Chili Dressing:
   - In a small bowl, whisk together lime juice, fish sauce, soy sauce, honey or maple syrup, chopped Thai bird's eye chilies, and minced garlic until well combined. Adjust the seasoning to taste.
3. Assemble the Salad:
   - Place the cooked eggplant slices or cubes in a serving dish.
   - Drizzle the chili dressing over the eggplants, ensuring they are evenly coated.

4. Garnish and Serve:
   - Sprinkle chopped fresh cilantro and chopped green onions over the salad.
   - If desired, garnish with chopped roasted peanuts for added texture and flavor.
   - Serve the Thai Eggplant Salad with Chili Dressing immediately as a flavorful appetizer or side dish.

Feel free to adjust the level of spiciness in the dressing according to your preference.

This salad can be served warm or at room temperature, making it perfect for any

occasion. Enjoy the vibrant flavors of Thai cuisine with this delicious eggplant salad!

Thai Green Papaya Salad with Shrimp

Ingredients:

For the Salad:

- 1 green papaya, peeled and julienned (or shredded)
- 1 cup cooked shrimp, peeled and deveined
- 1 cup cherry tomatoes, halved
- 1/2 cup green beans, trimmed and cut into 1-inch pieces
- 1/4 cup roasted peanuts, chopped
- 2 tablespoons dried shrimp (optional)
- 2-3 Thai bird's eye chilies, finely chopped (adjust to taste)
- 2 cloves garlic, minced
- 1/4 cup fresh lime juice
- 2 tablespoons fish sauce
- 1 tablespoon palm sugar or brown sugar
- 1 tablespoon tamarind paste (optional)
- 2 tablespoons chopped cilantro
- 2 tablespoons chopped mint leaves

Instructions:

1. Prepare the Green Papaya:
   - Peel the green papaya and cut it into thin julienne strips using a julienne peeler or a sharp knife. Alternatively, you can shred the papaya using a grater.
2. Cook the Shrimp:
   - If the shrimp are not already cooked, bring a pot of water to a boil. Add the shrimp and cook for 2-3 minutes until they turn pink and opaque. Drain and set aside to cool.
3. Make the Dressing:
   - In a small bowl, combine minced garlic, chopped Thai bird's eye chilies, lime juice, fish sauce, palm sugar, and tamarind paste (if using). Stir until the sugar is dissolved and the ingredients are well combined. Adjust the seasoning to taste.
4. Assemble the Salad:

- In a large mixing bowl, combine the julienned green papaya, cooked shrimp, halved cherry tomatoes, green beans, chopped roasted peanuts, and dried shrimp (if using).
- Pour the dressing over the salad and toss to coat everything evenly.
5. Garnish and Serve:
    - Garnish the salad with chopped cilantro and mint leaves.
    - Serve the Thai Green Papaya Salad with Shrimp immediately as a refreshing appetizer or light meal.

This Thai Green Papaya Salad with Shrimp is bursting with vibrant flavors and textures, making it a perfect dish for a summer day or any time you crave something refreshing and tangy. Enjoy!

Low-carb Thai Turkey Larb Salad

Ingredients:

For the Turkey Larb:

- 1 lb (450g) ground turkey
- 2 tablespoons vegetable oil
- 3 shallots, finely chopped
- 3 cloves garlic, minced
- 1-2 Thai bird's eye chilies, finely chopped (adjust to taste)
- 2 tablespoons fish sauce
- 2 tablespoons lime juice
- 1 tablespoon soy sauce or tamari (for gluten-free option)
- 1 teaspoon erythritol or monk fruit sweetener (optional)
- 1/4 cup fresh cilantro leaves, chopped
- 1/4 cup fresh mint leaves, chopped
- 2 green onions, thinly sliced
- Salt and pepper to taste

For the Salad:

- 4 cups mixed salad greens (such as lettuce, spinach, or arugula)
- 1 cucumber, thinly sliced
- 1/2 cup cherry tomatoes, halved
- 1/4 cup chopped peanuts or almonds (optional)
- Lime wedges for serving

Instructions:

1. Cook the Turkey Larb:
   - Heat vegetable oil in a skillet over medium-high heat. Add shallots, garlic, and Thai chilies. Sauté until fragrant, about 1-2 minutes.
   - Add the ground turkey to the skillet, breaking it up with a spoon. Cook until the turkey is browned and cooked through, about 5-7 minutes.
   - Stir in fish sauce, lime juice, soy sauce, and erythritol or monk fruit sweetener (if using). Cook for an additional 2-3 minutes.
   - Remove from heat and stir in chopped cilantro, chopped mint, and sliced green onions. Season with salt and pepper to taste.

2. Assemble the Salad:
   - In a large mixing bowl, combine the mixed salad greens, sliced cucumber, and halved cherry tomatoes.
   - Add the cooked turkey larb to the salad and toss to combine.
3. Garnish and Serve:
   - Sprinkle chopped peanuts or almonds over the salad for extra crunch and flavor.
   - Serve the low-carb Thai Turkey Larb Salad with lime wedges on the side for squeezing over the salad.

This low-carb Thai Turkey Larb Salad is packed with flavor and makes a satisfying meal on its own. Feel free to adjust the seasoning and spice level according to your preference. Enjoy!

Thai-style Grilled Fish Salad

Ingredients:

For the Grilled Fish:

- 1 lb (450g) firm white fish fillets (such as tilapia, cod, or snapper)
- 2 tablespoons fish sauce
- 2 tablespoons lime juice
- 1 tablespoon soy sauce or tamari (for gluten-free option)
- 1 tablespoon vegetable oil
- Salt and pepper to taste

For the Salad:

- 4 cups mixed salad greens (such as lettuce, spinach, or arugula)
- 1 cucumber, thinly sliced
- 1 red bell pepper, thinly sliced
- 1/2 red onion, thinly sliced
- 1/4 cup fresh cilantro leaves, chopped
- 1/4 cup fresh mint leaves, chopped
- 2-3 Thai bird's eye chilies, thinly sliced (adjust to taste)
- 1/4 cup roasted peanuts, chopped (optional)

For the Dressing:

- 3 tablespoons lime juice
- 2 tablespoons fish sauce
- 1 tablespoon soy sauce or tamari
- 1 tablespoon honey or maple syrup
- 1 tablespoon vegetable oil
- 2 cloves garlic, minced
- 1 Thai bird's eye chili, minced (adjust to taste)

Instructions:

1. Marinate and Grill the Fish:
   - In a shallow dish, whisk together fish sauce, lime juice, soy sauce, vegetable oil, salt, and pepper.

- Add the fish fillets to the marinade, turning to coat evenly. Let marinate for 15-30 minutes.
- Preheat the grill to medium-high heat. Grill the fish fillets for 3-4 minutes per side, or until cooked through and grill marks appear. Remove from the grill and let cool slightly.

2. Prepare the Salad:
   - In a large mixing bowl, combine the mixed salad greens, sliced cucumber, sliced red bell pepper, sliced red onion, chopped cilantro, chopped mint leaves, and sliced Thai bird's eye chilies.

3. Make the Dressing:
   - In a small bowl, whisk together lime juice, fish sauce, soy sauce, honey or maple syrup, vegetable oil, minced garlic, and minced Thai bird's eye chili until well combined.

4. Assemble the Salad:
   - Flake the grilled fish into bite-sized pieces and add to the salad.
   - Drizzle the dressing over the salad and gently toss to coat everything evenly.

5. Garnish and Serve:
   - If desired, sprinkle chopped roasted peanuts over the salad for added crunch and flavor.
   - Serve the Thai-style Grilled Fish Salad immediately as a light and flavorful meal.

Feel free to adjust the level of spiciness in the dressing by adding more or less Thai bird's eye chili according to your preference. Enjoy this vibrant and delicious Thai-inspired salad!

Thai Cucumber Salad with Peanut Dressing

Ingredients:

For the Salad:

- 2 large cucumbers, thinly sliced
- 1/2 red onion, thinly sliced
- 1/4 cup chopped cilantro
- 1/4 cup chopped peanuts, for garnish
- Lime wedges, for serving

For the Peanut Dressing:

- 1/4 cup creamy peanut butter
- 2 tablespoons rice vinegar
- 2 tablespoons soy sauce or tamari
- 1 tablespoon sesame oil
- 1 tablespoon honey or maple syrup
- 1 tablespoon lime juice
- 1 clove garlic, minced
- 1 teaspoon grated ginger
- 1 teaspoon sriracha sauce (adjust to taste)
- Water, as needed to thin the dressing
- Salt and pepper to taste

Instructions:

1. Prepare the Salad:
   - In a large mixing bowl, combine the thinly sliced cucumbers, thinly sliced red onion, and chopped cilantro. Toss gently to combine.
2. Make the Peanut Dressing:
   - In a small bowl, whisk together peanut butter, rice vinegar, soy sauce, sesame oil, honey or maple syrup, lime juice, minced garlic, grated ginger, and sriracha sauce until smooth.
   - If the dressing is too thick, gradually add water, a tablespoon at a time, until desired consistency is reached. Season with salt and pepper to taste.
3. Assemble the Salad:

- Drizzle the peanut dressing over the cucumber mixture in the large mixing bowl. Toss gently to coat the vegetables evenly with the dressing.
4. Garnish and Serve:
   - Transfer the Thai Cucumber Salad to a serving platter or individual plates.
   - Garnish with chopped peanuts and serve with lime wedges on the side for squeezing over the salad.

This Thai Cucumber Salad with Peanut Dressing is perfect as a side dish or as a light and refreshing appetizer. Enjoy the combination of crunchy cucumbers and creamy peanut dressing with hints of tangy, sweet, and spicy flavors!

Low-carb Thai Crab Salad with Lemongrass

Ingredients:

For the Salad:

- 1 lb (450g) fresh crab meat, cooked and shredded
- 2 stalks lemongrass, white parts only, finely chopped
- 1 cucumber, julienned
- 1 red bell pepper, thinly sliced
- 1/4 cup fresh cilantro leaves, chopped
- 1/4 cup fresh mint leaves, chopped
- 2 green onions, thinly sliced
- 1-2 Thai bird's eye chilies, thinly sliced (optional, adjust to taste)
- 1/4 cup chopped peanuts or almonds (optional, for garnish)

For the Dressing:

- 3 tablespoons lime juice
- 2 tablespoons fish sauce
- 1 tablespoon soy sauce or tamari (for gluten-free option)
- 1 tablespoon olive oil or sesame oil
- 1 tablespoon erythritol or monk fruit sweetener (optional)
- 1 clove garlic, minced
- 1 teaspoon grated ginger
- 1 teaspoon lemongrass paste or finely minced lemongrass
- Salt and pepper to taste

Instructions:

1. Prepare the Salad:
   - In a large mixing bowl, combine the shredded crab meat, chopped lemongrass, julienned cucumber, thinly sliced red bell pepper, chopped cilantro, chopped mint, sliced green onions, and sliced Thai bird's eye chilies (if using). Toss gently to combine.
2. Make the Dressing:
   - In a small bowl, whisk together lime juice, fish sauce, soy sauce, olive oil or sesame oil, erythritol or monk fruit sweetener (if using), minced garlic, grated ginger, minced lemongrass, salt, and pepper until well combined.

3. Assemble the Salad:
   - Pour the dressing over the crab salad mixture in the large mixing bowl. Toss gently to coat everything evenly with the dressing.
4. Garnish and Serve:
   - Transfer the low-carb Thai Crab Salad with Lemongrass to a serving platter or individual plates.
   - If desired, garnish with chopped peanuts or almonds for added crunch and flavor.

This low-carb Thai Crab Salad with Lemongrass is light, refreshing, and full of vibrant flavors. Enjoy the delicious combination of fresh crab meat and Thai-inspired dressing with hints of lemongrass, ginger, and herbs!

Thai-style Zucchini Noodle Salad

Ingredients:

For the Salad:

- 3 medium zucchinis, spiralized into noodles
- 1 carrot, julienned or grated
- 1 red bell pepper, thinly sliced
- 1/2 cup shredded purple cabbage
- 1/4 cup chopped cilantro
- 1/4 cup chopped mint leaves
- 1/4 cup chopped roasted peanuts or almonds (optional, for garnish)

For the Dressing:

- 3 tablespoons lime juice
- 2 tablespoons fish sauce
- 1 tablespoon soy sauce or tamari (for gluten-free option)
- 1 tablespoon sesame oil
- 1 tablespoon honey or maple syrup
- 1 clove garlic, minced
- 1 Thai bird's eye chili, minced (optional, adjust to taste)

Instructions:

1. Prepare the Zucchini Noodles:
   - Use a spiralizer to spiralize the zucchinis into noodles. If you don't have a spiralizer, you can use a julienne peeler to create long, thin strips resembling noodles.
2. Prepare the Dressing:
   - In a small bowl, whisk together lime juice, fish sauce, soy sauce, sesame oil, honey or maple syrup, minced garlic, and minced Thai bird's eye chili (if using) until well combined.
3. Assemble the Salad:
   - In a large mixing bowl, combine the zucchini noodles, julienned carrot, thinly sliced red bell pepper, shredded purple cabbage, chopped cilantro, and chopped mint leaves.
4. Add the Dressing:

- Pour the dressing over the salad ingredients in the mixing bowl. Toss gently to coat everything evenly with the dressing.
5. Garnish and Serve:
   - Transfer the Thai-style Zucchini Noodle Salad to a serving platter or individual plates.
   - If desired, garnish with chopped roasted peanuts or almonds for added crunch and flavor.

This Thai-style Zucchini Noodle Salad is light, flavorful, and perfect for a refreshing meal or side dish. Enjoy the combination of fresh vegetables and herbs with the tangy and savory dressing!

Low-carb Thai Beef Larb Lettuce Wraps

Ingredients:

For the Beef Larb:

- 1 lb (450g) ground beef
- 2 tablespoons vegetable oil
- 3 shallots, finely chopped
- 3 cloves garlic, minced
- 1-2 Thai bird's eye chilies, finely chopped (adjust to taste)
- 2 tablespoons fish sauce
- 2 tablespoons lime juice
- 1 tablespoon soy sauce or tamari (for gluten-free option)
- 1 teaspoon erythritol or monk fruit sweetener (optional)
- 1/4 cup fresh cilantro leaves, chopped
- 1/4 cup fresh mint leaves, chopped
- 2 green onions, thinly sliced
- Salt and pepper to taste

For the Lettuce Wraps:

- 1 head iceberg lettuce or butter lettuce, leaves separated
- Thinly sliced cucumber, for serving
- Thinly sliced red onion, for serving
- Lime wedges, for serving

Instructions:

1. Cook the Beef Larb:
   - Heat vegetable oil in a skillet over medium-high heat. Add shallots, garlic, and Thai chilies. Sauté until fragrant, about 1-2 minutes.
   - Add the ground beef to the skillet, breaking it up with a spoon. Cook until the beef is browned and cooked through, about 5-7 minutes.
   - Stir in fish sauce, lime juice, soy sauce, and erythritol or monk fruit sweetener (if using). Cook for an additional 2-3 minutes.
   - Remove from heat and stir in chopped cilantro, chopped mint, and sliced green onions. Season with salt and pepper to taste.
2. Prepare the Lettuce Wraps:

- Wash and dry the lettuce leaves. Arrange them on a serving platter.
- Place a spoonful of the cooked beef larb onto each lettuce leaf.
3. Assemble the Lettuce Wraps:
   - Top the beef larb with thinly sliced cucumber and red onion.
   - Serve the lettuce wraps with lime wedges on the side for squeezing over the filling.

These Low-carb Thai Beef Larb Lettuce Wraps are a flavorful and satisfying dish that's perfect for a light and healthy meal. Enjoy the combination of savory beef larb with the freshness of lettuce and crunchy vegetables!

Thai-style Cauliflower Rice Salad with Chicken

Ingredients:

For the Beef Larb:

- 1 lb (450g) ground beef
- 2 tablespoons vegetable oil
- 3 shallots, finely chopped
- 3 cloves garlic, minced
- 1-2 Thai bird's eye chilies, finely chopped (adjust to taste)
- 2 tablespoons fish sauce
- 2 tablespoons lime juice
- 1 tablespoon soy sauce or tamari (for gluten-free option)
- 1 teaspoon erythritol or monk fruit sweetener (optional)
- 1/4 cup fresh cilantro leaves, chopped
- 1/4 cup fresh mint leaves, chopped
- 2 green onions, thinly sliced
- Salt and pepper to taste

For the Lettuce Wraps:

- 1 head iceberg lettuce or butter lettuce, leaves separated
- Thinly sliced cucumber, for serving
- Thinly sliced red onion, for serving
- Lime wedges, for serving

Instructions:

1. Cook the Beef Larb:
    - Heat vegetable oil in a skillet over medium-high heat. Add shallots, garlic, and Thai chilies. Sauté until fragrant, about 1-2 minutes.
    - Add the ground beef to the skillet, breaking it up with a spoon. Cook until the beef is browned and cooked through, about 5-7 minutes.
    - Stir in fish sauce, lime juice, soy sauce, and erythritol or monk fruit sweetener (if using). Cook for an additional 2-3 minutes.
    - Remove from heat and stir in chopped cilantro, chopped mint, and sliced green onions. Season with salt and pepper to taste.
2. Prepare the Lettuce Wraps:

- Wash and dry the lettuce leaves. Arrange them on a serving platter.
- Place a spoonful of the cooked beef larb onto each lettuce leaf.

3. Assemble the Lettuce Wraps:
   - Top the beef larb with thinly sliced cucumber and red onion.
   - Serve the lettuce wraps with lime wedges on the side for squeezing over the filling.

These Low-carb Thai Beef Larb Lettuce Wraps are a flavorful and satisfying dish that's perfect for a light and healthy meal. Enjoy the combination of savory beef larb with the freshness of lettuce and crunchy vegetables!

Thai-style Cauliflower Rice Salad with Chicken

Ingredients:

For the Cauliflower Rice Salad:

- 1 medium head cauliflower, grated into rice-like texture
- 2 cups cooked chicken breast, shredded or diced
- 1 red bell pepper, thinly sliced
- 1 carrot, julienned or grated
- 1/2 cucumber, thinly sliced
- 1/4 cup chopped cilantro
- 1/4 cup chopped mint leaves
- 1/4 cup chopped roasted peanuts or almonds (optional, for garnish)

For the Dressing:

- 3 tablespoons lime juice
- 2 tablespoons fish sauce
- 1 tablespoon soy sauce or tamari (for gluten-free option)
- 1 tablespoon sesame oil
- 1 tablespoon honey or maple syrup
- 1 clove garlic, minced
- 1 Thai bird's eye chili, minced (adjust to taste)

Instructions:

1. Prepare the Cauliflower Rice:
   - Wash and dry the cauliflower. Cut it into florets and then grate them using a box grater or pulse them in a food processor until they resemble rice.
2. Cook the Chicken:
   - If the chicken breast is not already cooked, you can poach or grill it until fully cooked. Let it cool, then shred or dice it into bite-sized pieces.
3. Prepare the Dressing:
   - In a small bowl, whisk together lime juice, fish sauce, soy sauce, sesame oil, honey or maple syrup, minced garlic, and minced Thai bird's eye chili until well combined.
4. Assemble the Salad:

- In a large mixing bowl, combine the cauliflower rice, cooked chicken breast, sliced red bell pepper, julienned carrot, sliced cucumber, chopped cilantro, and chopped mint leaves.
5. Add the Dressing:
   - Pour the dressing over the salad ingredients in the mixing bowl. Toss gently to coat everything evenly with the dressing.
6. Garnish and Serve:
   - Transfer the Thai-style Cauliflower Rice Salad with Chicken to a serving platter or individual plates.
   - If desired, garnish with chopped roasted peanuts or almonds for added crunch and flavor.

This Thai-style Cauliflower Rice Salad with Chicken is light, refreshing, and packed with flavor. Enjoy the delicious combination of cauliflower rice, chicken, and Thai-inspired dressing with hints of lime, fish sauce, and chili!

Low-carb Thai Chicken Larb Lettuce Cups

Ingredients:

For the Chicken Larb:

- 1 lb (450g) ground chicken
- 2 tablespoons vegetable oil
- 3 shallots, finely chopped
- 3 cloves garlic, minced
- 1-2 Thai bird's eye chilies, finely chopped (adjust to taste)
- 2 tablespoons fish sauce
- 2 tablespoons lime juice
- 1 tablespoon soy sauce or tamari (for gluten-free option)
- 1 teaspoon erythritol or monk fruit sweetener (optional)
- 1/4 cup fresh cilantro leaves, chopped
- 1/4 cup fresh mint leaves, chopped
- 2 green onions, thinly sliced
- Salt and pepper to taste

For the Lettuce Cups:

- 1 head iceberg lettuce or butter lettuce, leaves separated
- Thinly sliced cucumber, for serving
- Thinly sliced red onion, for serving
- Lime wedges, for serving

Instructions:

1. Cook the Chicken Larb:
   - Heat vegetable oil in a skillet over medium-high heat. Add shallots, garlic, and Thai chilies. Sauté until fragrant, about 1-2 minutes.
   - Add the ground chicken to the skillet, breaking it up with a spoon. Cook until the chicken is browned and cooked through, about 5-7 minutes.
   - Stir in fish sauce, lime juice, soy sauce, and erythritol or monk fruit sweetener (if using). Cook for an additional 2-3 minutes.
   - Remove from heat and stir in chopped cilantro, chopped mint, and sliced green onions. Season with salt and pepper to taste.
2. Prepare the Lettuce Cups:

- Wash and dry the lettuce leaves. Arrange them on a serving platter.
3. Assemble the Lettuce Cups:
    - Spoon the chicken larb mixture into each lettuce cup.
    - Top with thinly sliced cucumber and red onion.
4. Serve:
    - Serve the low-carb Thai Chicken Larb Lettuce Cups with lime wedges on the side for squeezing over the filling.

These low-carb Thai Chicken Larb Lettuce Cups are a flavorful and satisfying dish that's perfect for a light and healthy meal. Enjoy the savory chicken larb with the crisp freshness of lettuce and crunchy vegetables!

Thai-inspired Spicy Beef Salad with Mint

Ingredients:

For the Beef Salad:

- 1 lb (450g) beef steak (such as sirloin or flank), thinly sliced
- 2 tablespoons vegetable oil
- Salt and pepper to taste
- 4 cups mixed salad greens (such as lettuce, spinach, or arugula)
- 1 cucumber, thinly sliced
- 1 red onion, thinly sliced
- 1/4 cup fresh mint leaves, chopped
- 1/4 cup fresh cilantro leaves, chopped
- 1/4 cup chopped roasted peanuts (optional, for garnish)

For the Dressing:

- 3 tablespoons lime juice
- 2 tablespoons fish sauce
- 1 tablespoon soy sauce or tamari (for gluten-free option)
- 1 tablespoon honey or maple syrup
- 1 tablespoon sesame oil
- 1-2 Thai bird's eye chilies, finely chopped (adjust to taste)
- 2 cloves garlic, minced

Instructions:

1. Marinate and Cook the Beef:
   - Season the beef slices with salt and pepper.
   - Heat vegetable oil in a skillet over medium-high heat. Add the beef slices and cook for 2-3 minutes per side until browned and cooked to your desired doneness. Remove from heat and let it rest for a few minutes. Then, thinly slice the cooked beef against the grain.
2. Prepare the Dressing:
   - In a small bowl, whisk together lime juice, fish sauce, soy sauce, honey or maple syrup, sesame oil, minced Thai bird's eye chilies, and minced garlic until well combined.
3. Assemble the Salad:

- In a large mixing bowl, combine the mixed salad greens, thinly sliced cucumber, thinly sliced red onion, chopped mint leaves, and chopped cilantro leaves.
- Add the sliced cooked beef to the salad.

4. Add the Dressing:
   - Drizzle the dressing over the salad ingredients in the mixing bowl. Toss gently to coat everything evenly with the dressing.
5. Garnish and Serve:
   - Transfer the Thai-inspired Spicy Beef Salad with Mint to a serving platter or individual plates.
   - If desired, garnish with chopped roasted peanuts for added crunch and flavor.

This Thai-inspired Spicy Beef Salad with Mint is a delicious and refreshing dish that's perfect for a light and flavorful meal. Enjoy the tender beef slices with the aromatic herbs and spicy dressing!

Low-carb Thai Tofu Larb Lettuce Wraps

Ingredients:

For the Tofu Larb:

- 14 oz (400g) extra-firm tofu, pressed and crumbled
- 2 tablespoons vegetable oil
- 3 shallots, finely chopped
- 3 cloves garlic, minced
- 1-2 Thai bird's eye chilies, finely chopped (adjust to taste)
- 2 tablespoons fish sauce
- 2 tablespoons lime juice
- 1 tablespoon soy sauce or tamari (for gluten-free option)
- 1 teaspoon erythritol or monk fruit sweetener (optional)
- 1/4 cup fresh cilantro leaves, chopped
- 1/4 cup fresh mint leaves, chopped
- 2 green onions, thinly sliced
- Salt and pepper to taste

For the Lettuce Wraps:

- 1 head iceberg lettuce or butter lettuce, leaves separated
- Thinly sliced cucumber, for serving
- Thinly sliced red onion, for serving
- Lime wedges, for serving

Instructions:

1. Prepare the Tofu Larb:
   - Press the tofu to remove excess moisture, then crumble it into small pieces.
   - Heat vegetable oil in a skillet over medium-high heat. Add shallots, garlic, and Thai chilies. Sauté until fragrant, about 1-2 minutes.
   - Add the crumbled tofu to the skillet. Cook until the tofu is lightly browned and slightly crispy, about 5-7 minutes.
   - Stir in fish sauce, lime juice, soy sauce, and erythritol or monk fruit sweetener (if using). Cook for an additional 2-3 minutes.

- Remove from heat and stir in chopped cilantro, chopped mint, and sliced green onions. Season with salt and pepper to taste.
2. Prepare the Lettuce Wraps:
   - Wash and dry the lettuce leaves. Arrange them on a serving platter.
3. Assemble the Lettuce Wraps:
   - Spoon the tofu larb mixture into each lettuce cup.
   - Top with thinly sliced cucumber and red onion.
4. Serve:
   - Serve the low-carb Thai Tofu Larb Lettuce Wraps with lime wedges on the side for squeezing over the filling.

These low-carb Thai Tofu Larb Lettuce Wraps are flavorful, satisfying, and perfect for a light and healthy meal. Enjoy the savory tofu larb with the crisp freshness of lettuce and crunchy vegetables!

Thai-style Grilled Chicken and Vegetable Salad

Ingredients:

For the Grilled Chicken:

- 2 boneless, skinless chicken breasts
- 2 tablespoons soy sauce or tamari (for gluten-free option)
- 1 tablespoon fish sauce
- 1 tablespoon lime juice
- 1 tablespoon honey or maple syrup
- 2 cloves garlic, minced
- 1 teaspoon grated ginger
- 1 teaspoon sesame oil
- Salt and pepper to taste

For the Salad:

- 2 cups mixed salad greens (such as lettuce, spinach, or arugula)
- 1 cucumber, thinly sliced
- 1 red bell pepper, thinly sliced
- 1 carrot, julienned or grated
- 1/2 red onion, thinly sliced
- 1/4 cup fresh cilantro leaves, chopped
- 1/4 cup fresh mint leaves, chopped
- 1/4 cup chopped roasted peanuts or almonds (optional, for garnish)

For the Dressing:

- 3 tablespoons lime juice
- 2 tablespoons fish sauce
- 1 tablespoon soy sauce or tamari
- 1 tablespoon honey or maple syrup
- 1 tablespoon vegetable oil
- 1-2 Thai bird's eye chilies, finely chopped (adjust to taste)
- 2 cloves garlic, minced
- 1 teaspoon grated ginger

Instructions:

1. Marinate and Grill the Chicken:
   - In a bowl, whisk together soy sauce, fish sauce, lime juice, honey or maple syrup, minced garlic, grated ginger, sesame oil, salt, and pepper to make the marinade.
   - Add the chicken breasts to the marinade, turning to coat evenly. Let marinate for at least 30 minutes in the refrigerator.
   - Preheat the grill or grill pan over medium-high heat. Grill the chicken breasts for 6-8 minutes per side, or until cooked through and grill marks appear. Remove from heat and let rest for a few minutes before slicing.
2. Prepare the Salad:
   - In a large mixing bowl, combine the mixed salad greens, thinly sliced cucumber, thinly sliced red bell pepper, julienned or grated carrot, thinly sliced red onion, chopped cilantro, and chopped mint leaves.
3. Make the Dressing:
   - In a small bowl, whisk together lime juice, fish sauce, soy sauce, honey or maple syrup, vegetable oil, chopped Thai bird's eye chilies, minced garlic, and grated ginger until well combined.
4. Assemble the Salad:
   - Add the sliced grilled chicken to the salad mixture in the large mixing bowl.
   - Drizzle the dressing over the salad and toss gently to coat everything evenly.
5. Garnish and Serve:
   - If desired, garnish the Thai-style Grilled Chicken and Vegetable Salad with chopped roasted peanuts or almonds for added crunch and flavor.
   - Serve immediately as a delicious and vibrant main dish or light meal.

Enjoy the burst of flavors and textures in this Thai-style Grilled Chicken and Vegetable Salad, perfect for a refreshing and satisfying meal!

Low-carb Thai Pork Larb Lettuce Wraps

Ingredients:

For the Pork Larb:

- 1 lb (450g) ground pork
- 2 tablespoons vegetable oil
- 3 shallots, finely chopped
- 3 cloves garlic, minced
- 1-2 Thai bird's eye chilies, finely chopped (adjust to taste)
- 2 tablespoons fish sauce
- 2 tablespoons lime juice
- 1 tablespoon soy sauce or tamari (for gluten-free option)
- 1 teaspoon erythritol or monk fruit sweetener (optional)
- 1/4 cup fresh cilantro leaves, chopped
- 1/4 cup fresh mint leaves, chopped
- 2 green onions, thinly sliced
- Salt and pepper to taste

For the Lettuce Wraps:

- 1 head iceberg lettuce or butter lettuce, leaves separated
- Thinly sliced cucumber, for serving
- Thinly sliced red onion, for serving
- Lime wedges, for serving

Instructions:

1. Cook the Pork Larb:
   - Heat vegetable oil in a skillet over medium-high heat. Add shallots, garlic, and Thai chilies. Sauté until fragrant, about 1-2 minutes.
   - Add the ground pork to the skillet. Cook until the pork is browned and cooked through, breaking it up with a spoon, about 5-7 minutes.
   - Stir in fish sauce, lime juice, soy sauce, and erythritol or monk fruit sweetener (if using). Cook for an additional 2-3 minutes.
   - Remove from heat and stir in chopped cilantro, chopped mint, and sliced green onions. Season with salt and pepper to taste.
2. Prepare the Lettuce Wraps:

- Wash and dry the lettuce leaves. Arrange them on a serving platter.
3. Assemble the Lettuce Wraps:
   - Spoon the pork larb mixture into each lettuce cup.
   - Top with thinly sliced cucumber and red onion.
4. Serve:
   - Serve the low-carb Thai Pork Larb Lettuce Wraps with lime wedges on the side for squeezing over the filling.

These low-carb Thai Pork Larb Lettuce Wraps are a flavorful and satisfying dish that's perfect for a light and healthy meal. Enjoy the savory pork larb with the crisp freshness of lettuce and crunchy vegetables!

Thai-inspired Cabbage Salad with Spicy Dressing

Ingredients:

For the Salad:

- 1/2 head of green cabbage, thinly shredded
- 1/2 head of purple cabbage, thinly shredded
- 1 carrot, grated
- 1 red bell pepper, thinly sliced
- 1/2 cup fresh cilantro leaves, chopped
- 1/4 cup fresh mint leaves, chopped
- 1/4 cup chopped roasted peanuts or cashews (optional, for garnish)

For the Spicy Dressing:

- 3 tablespoons lime juice
- 2 tablespoons fish sauce
- 1 tablespoon soy sauce or tamari (for gluten-free option)
- 1 tablespoon honey or maple syrup
- 1 tablespoon vegetable oil
- 1-2 Thai bird's eye chilies, finely chopped (adjust to taste)
- 2 cloves garlic, minced
- 1 teaspoon grated ginger

Instructions:

1. Prepare the Salad:
   - In a large mixing bowl, combine the thinly shredded green cabbage, purple cabbage, grated carrot, thinly sliced red bell pepper, chopped cilantro, and chopped mint leaves. Toss gently to combine.
2. Make the Spicy Dressing:
   - In a small bowl, whisk together lime juice, fish sauce, soy sauce, honey or maple syrup, vegetable oil, chopped Thai bird's eye chilies, minced garlic, and grated ginger until well combined.
3. Dress the Salad:
   - Pour the spicy dressing over the cabbage salad mixture in the large mixing bowl. Toss gently to coat everything evenly with the dressing.
4. Garnish and Serve:

- Transfer the Thai-inspired Cabbage Salad with Spicy Dressing to a serving platter or individual plates.
- If desired, garnish with chopped roasted peanuts or cashews for added crunch and flavor.

This Thai-inspired Cabbage Salad with Spicy Dressing is a refreshing and vibrant dish that pairs well with grilled meats or as a light and flavorful meal on its own. Enjoy the combination of crunchy cabbage and zesty, spicy dressing!

Low-carb Thai Shrimp Larb Lettuce Cups

Ingredients:

For the Shrimp Larb:

- 1 lb (450g) shrimp, peeled and deveined
- 2 tablespoons vegetable oil
- 3 shallots, finely chopped
- 3 cloves garlic, minced
- 1-2 Thai bird's eye chilies, finely chopped (adjust to taste)
- 2 tablespoons fish sauce
- 2 tablespoons lime juice
- 1 tablespoon soy sauce or tamari (for gluten-free option)
- 1 teaspoon erythritol or monk fruit sweetener (optional)
- 1/4 cup fresh cilantro leaves, chopped
- 1/4 cup fresh mint leaves, chopped
- 2 green onions, thinly sliced
- Salt and pepper to taste

For the Lettuce Cups:

- 1 head iceberg lettuce or butter lettuce, leaves separated
- Thinly sliced cucumber, for serving
- Thinly sliced red onion, for serving
- Lime wedges, for serving

Instructions:

1. Cook the Shrimp Larb:
   - Heat vegetable oil in a skillet over medium-high heat. Add shallots, garlic, and Thai chilies. Sauté until fragrant, about 1-2 minutes.
   - Add the shrimp to the skillet. Cook until the shrimp are pink and cooked through, about 2-3 minutes.
   - Stir in fish sauce, lime juice, soy sauce, and erythritol or monk fruit sweetener (if using). Cook for an additional 1-2 minutes.
   - Remove from heat and stir in chopped cilantro, chopped mint, and sliced green onions. Season with salt and pepper to taste.
2. Prepare the Lettuce Cups:

- Wash and dry the lettuce leaves. Arrange them on a serving platter.
3. Assemble the Lettuce Cups:
   - Spoon the shrimp larb mixture into each lettuce cup.
   - Top with thinly sliced cucumber and red onion.
4. Serve:
   - Serve the low-carb Thai Shrimp Larb Lettuce Cups with lime wedges on the side for squeezing over the filling.

These low-carb Thai Shrimp Larb Lettuce Cups are a flavorful and satisfying dish that's perfect for a light and healthy meal. Enjoy the savory shrimp larb with the crisp freshness of lettuce and crunchy vegetables!

Thai-style Grilled Eggplant Salad with Sesame Dressing

Ingredients:

For the Grilled Eggplant:

- 2 large eggplants, sliced lengthwise into 1/2-inch thick slices
- 2 tablespoons olive oil
- Salt and pepper to taste

For the Sesame Dressing:

- 3 tablespoons sesame oil
- 2 tablespoons rice vinegar
- 1 tablespoon soy sauce or tamari (for gluten-free option)
- 1 tablespoon honey or maple syrup
- 1 clove garlic, minced
- 1 teaspoon grated ginger
- 1 teaspoon sesame seeds

For the Salad:

- 1 red bell pepper, thinly sliced
- 1/4 cup chopped green onions
- 2 tablespoons chopped fresh cilantro
- 2 tablespoons chopped fresh mint
- 2 tablespoons chopped roasted peanuts or almonds (optional, for garnish)

Instructions:

1. Grill the Eggplant:
   - Preheat the grill to medium-high heat. Brush both sides of the eggplant slices with olive oil and season with salt and pepper.
   - Grill the eggplant slices for 4-5 minutes per side, or until tender and charred grill marks appear. Remove from the grill and let cool slightly.
2. Make the Sesame Dressing:
   - In a small bowl, whisk together sesame oil, rice vinegar, soy sauce, honey or maple syrup, minced garlic, grated ginger, and sesame seeds until well combined.
3. Assemble the Salad:

- Cut the grilled eggplant slices into bite-sized pieces and place them in a large mixing bowl.
- Add the thinly sliced red bell pepper, chopped green onions, chopped cilantro, and chopped mint to the bowl with the grilled eggplant.

4. Add the Dressing:
   - Pour the sesame dressing over the salad ingredients in the mixing bowl. Toss gently to coat everything evenly with the dressing.

5. Garnish and Serve:
   - Transfer the Thai-style Grilled Eggplant Salad with Sesame Dressing to a serving platter or individual plates.
   - If desired, garnish with chopped roasted peanuts or almonds for added crunch and flavor.

This Thai-style Grilled Eggplant Salad with Sesame Dressing is a vibrant and flavorful dish that's perfect as a side dish or light meal. Enjoy the combination of smoky grilled eggplant with the tangy sesame dressing and fresh herbs!

Low-carb Thai Turkey Larb Lettuce Wraps

Ingredients:

For the Turkey Larb:

- 1 lb (450g) ground turkey
- 2 tablespoons vegetable oil
- 3 shallots, finely chopped
- 3 cloves garlic, minced
- 1-2 Thai bird's eye chilies, finely chopped (adjust to taste)
- 2 tablespoons fish sauce
- 2 tablespoons lime juice
- 1 tablespoon soy sauce or tamari (for gluten-free option)
- 1 teaspoon erythritol or monk fruit sweetener (optional)
- 1/4 cup fresh cilantro leaves, chopped
- 1/4 cup fresh mint leaves, chopped
- 2 green onions, thinly sliced
- Salt and pepper to taste

For the Lettuce Wraps:

- 1 head iceberg lettuce or butter lettuce, leaves separated
- Thinly sliced cucumber, for serving
- Thinly sliced red onion, for serving
- Lime wedges, for serving

Instructions:

1. Cook the Turkey Larb:
   - Heat vegetable oil in a skillet over medium-high heat. Add shallots, garlic, and Thai chilies. Sauté until fragrant, about 1-2 minutes.
   - Add the ground turkey to the skillet. Cook until the turkey is browned and cooked through, breaking it up with a spoon, about 5-7 minutes.
   - Stir in fish sauce, lime juice, soy sauce, and erythritol or monk fruit sweetener (if using). Cook for an additional 2-3 minutes.
   - Remove from heat and stir in chopped cilantro, chopped mint, and sliced green onions. Season with salt and pepper to taste.
2. Prepare the Lettuce Wraps:

- Wash and dry the lettuce leaves. Arrange them on a serving platter.
3. Assemble the Lettuce Wraps:
    - Spoon the turkey larb mixture into each lettuce cup.
    - Top with thinly sliced cucumber and red onion.
4. Serve:
    - Serve the low-carb Thai Turkey Larb Lettuce Wraps with lime wedges on the side for squeezing over the filling.

These low-carb Thai Turkey Larb Lettuce Wraps are a delicious and healthy alternative to traditional larb. Enjoy the savory turkey larb with the crisp freshness of lettuce and crunchy vegetables!

Thai-inspired Broccoli Salad with Peanut Dressing

Ingredients:

For the Broccoli Salad:

- 1 large head of broccoli, cut into small florets
- 1/2 red bell pepper, thinly sliced
- 1/2 yellow bell pepper, thinly sliced
- 1/4 cup shredded carrots
- 1/4 cup chopped fresh cilantro
- 1/4 cup chopped roasted peanuts (for garnish)

For the Peanut Dressing:

- 1/4 cup creamy peanut butter
- 2 tablespoons soy sauce or tamari (for gluten-free option)
- 2 tablespoons rice vinegar
- 1 tablespoon sesame oil
- 1 tablespoon honey or maple syrup
- 1 clove garlic, minced
- 1 teaspoon grated ginger
- 2-3 tablespoons water, to thin the dressing
- Red pepper flakes, to taste (optional, for added heat)

Instructions:

1. Blanch the Broccoli:
    - Bring a large pot of salted water to a boil. Add the broccoli florets and cook for 1-2 minutes, until slightly tender but still crisp. Drain the broccoli and immediately transfer to a bowl of ice water to stop the cooking process. Drain again and pat dry with paper towels.
2. Prepare the Salad:
    - In a large mixing bowl, combine the blanched broccoli florets, thinly sliced red and yellow bell peppers, shredded carrots, and chopped cilantro.
3. Make the Peanut Dressing:
    - In a small bowl, whisk together the creamy peanut butter, soy sauce or tamari, rice vinegar, sesame oil, honey or maple syrup, minced garlic, and grated ginger until smooth. If the dressing is too thick, add water, one

tablespoon at a time, until desired consistency is reached. Add red pepper flakes to taste for added heat, if desired.

4. Toss the Salad with Dressing:
   - Pour the peanut dressing over the broccoli salad mixture in the large mixing bowl. Toss gently until all the ingredients are evenly coated with the dressing.
5. Garnish and Serve:
   - Transfer the Thai-inspired Broccoli Salad with Peanut Dressing to a serving dish or individual plates.
   - Garnish with chopped roasted peanuts for added crunch and flavor.

This Thai-inspired Broccoli Salad with Peanut Dressing is a vibrant and flavorful dish that's perfect as a side dish or light meal. Enjoy the combination of crunchy broccoli florets and creamy peanut dressing!

Low-carb Thai Beef Salad with Cucumber Ribbons

Ingredients:

For the Beef:

- 1 lb (450g) beef sirloin or flank steak, thinly sliced
- 2 tablespoons soy sauce or tamari (for gluten-free option)
- 2 tablespoons fish sauce
- 1 tablespoon lime juice
- 1 tablespoon sesame oil
- 2 cloves garlic, minced
- 1 teaspoon grated ginger
- 1 teaspoon erythritol or monk fruit sweetener (optional)
- Salt and pepper to taste

For the Salad:

- 2 medium cucumbers
- 1 red bell pepper, thinly sliced
- 1/4 cup fresh cilantro leaves, chopped
- 1/4 cup fresh mint leaves, chopped
- 2 green onions, thinly sliced
- 2 tablespoons chopped roasted peanuts (optional, for garnish)

For the Dressing:

- 3 tablespoons lime juice
- 2 tablespoons fish sauce
- 1 tablespoon soy sauce or tamari
- 1 tablespoon sesame oil
- 1 tablespoon erythritol or monk fruit sweetener (optional)
- 1 Thai bird's eye chili, finely chopped (adjust to taste)
- 2 cloves garlic, minced
- 1 teaspoon grated ginger

Instructions:

1. Marinate the Beef:

- In a bowl, whisk together soy sauce, fish sauce, lime juice, sesame oil, minced garlic, grated ginger, erythritol or monk fruit sweetener (if using), salt, and pepper to make the marinade.
- Add the thinly sliced beef to the marinade, turning to coat evenly. Let marinate for at least 30 minutes in the refrigerator.

2. Prepare the Cucumber Ribbons:
   - Use a vegetable peeler to create long ribbons from the cucumbers. Start at one end and peel lengthwise until you reach the seeds. Rotate the cucumber and continue peeling until you have created ribbons from all sides.

3. Grill the Beef:
   - Preheat a grill or grill pan over medium-high heat. Remove the beef from the marinade and discard any excess marinade.
   - Grill the beef slices for 1-2 minutes per side, or until cooked to your desired level of doneness. Remove from heat and let rest for a few minutes.

4. Assemble the Salad:
   - In a large mixing bowl, combine the cucumber ribbons, thinly sliced red bell pepper, chopped cilantro, chopped mint, and sliced green onions.
   - Slice the grilled beef into thin strips and add it to the salad mixture.

5. Make the Dressing:
   - In a small bowl, whisk together lime juice, fish sauce, soy sauce, sesame oil, erythritol or monk fruit sweetener (if using), chopped Thai bird's eye chili, minced garlic, and grated ginger until well combined.

6. Toss with Dressing:
   - Pour the dressing over the salad ingredients in the mixing bowl. Toss gently to coat everything evenly with the dressing.

7. Garnish and Serve:
   - Transfer the Low-carb Thai Beef Salad with Cucumber Ribbons to a serving platter or individual plates.
   - If desired, garnish with chopped roasted peanuts for added crunch and flavor.

This Low-carb Thai Beef Salad with Cucumber Ribbons is a delicious and refreshing dish that's perfect for a light and healthy meal. Enjoy the tender grilled beef with the crisp freshness of cucumber ribbons and zesty dressing!

Thai-style Seared Tuna Salad with Spicy Dressing

Ingredients:

For the Seared Tuna:

- 2 tuna steaks (about 6 oz each)
- 1 tablespoon soy sauce or tamari (for gluten-free option)
- 1 tablespoon sesame oil
- 1 teaspoon grated ginger
- 1 teaspoon sesame seeds
- Salt and pepper to taste

For the Salad:

- 4 cups mixed salad greens (such as lettuce, spinach, or arugula)
- 1 cucumber, thinly sliced
- 1 carrot, julienned or grated
- 1/2 red bell pepper, thinly sliced
- 1/2 yellow bell pepper, thinly sliced
- 1/4 cup chopped fresh cilantro
- 1/4 cup chopped fresh mint
- 2 green onions, thinly sliced

For the Spicy Dressing:

- 3 tablespoons lime juice
- 2 tablespoons fish sauce
- 1 tablespoon soy sauce or tamari
- 1 tablespoon sesame oil
- 1 tablespoon honey or maple syrup
- 1 Thai bird's eye chili, finely chopped (adjust to taste)
- 2 cloves garlic, minced
- 1 teaspoon grated ginger

For Garnish:

- Chopped roasted peanuts or cashews
- Lime wedges

Instructions:

1. Marinate the Tuna:
   - In a shallow dish, whisk together soy sauce, sesame oil, grated ginger, sesame seeds, salt, and pepper. Add the tuna steaks to the marinade, turning to coat evenly. Let marinate for 15-30 minutes in the refrigerator.
2. Prepare the Salad Ingredients:
   - In a large mixing bowl, combine the mixed salad greens, thinly sliced cucumber, julienned or grated carrot, thinly sliced red and yellow bell peppers, chopped cilantro, chopped mint, and sliced green onions. Toss gently to combine.
3. Make the Spicy Dressing:
   - In a small bowl, whisk together lime juice, fish sauce, soy sauce, sesame oil, honey or maple syrup, chopped Thai bird's eye chili, minced garlic, and grated ginger until well combined. Adjust seasoning to taste.
4. Sear the Tuna:
   - Heat a skillet or grill pan over high heat. Remove the tuna steaks from the marinade and discard any excess marinade.
   - Sear the tuna steaks for 1-2 minutes per side, or until browned on the outside and rare to medium-rare on the inside. Cooking time will vary depending on the thickness of the tuna steaks. Do not overcook.
5. Assemble the Salad:
   - Divide the prepared salad mixture among serving plates.
   - Slice the seared tuna steaks thinly and arrange them on top of the salad.
6. Drizzle with Dressing:
   - Drizzle the spicy dressing over the seared tuna and salad.
7. Garnish and Serve:
   - Garnish with chopped roasted peanuts or cashews and serve with lime wedges on the side.

This Thai-style Seared Tuna Salad with Spicy Dressing is a delicious and satisfying dish that's perfect for a light and flavorful meal. Enjoy the combination of tender seared tuna, crisp vegetables, and zesty dressing!

Low-carb Thai Chicken Larb Salad with Lettuce Wraps

Ingredients:

For the Chicken Larb:

- 1 lb (450g) ground chicken
- 2 tablespoons vegetable oil
- 3 shallots, finely chopped
- 3 cloves garlic, minced
- 1-2 Thai bird's eye chilies, finely chopped (adjust to taste)
- 2 tablespoons fish sauce
- 2 tablespoons lime juice
- 1 tablespoon soy sauce or tamari (for gluten-free option)
- 1 teaspoon erythritol or monk fruit sweetener (optional)
- 1/4 cup fresh cilantro leaves, chopped
- 1/4 cup fresh mint leaves, chopped
- 2 green onions, thinly sliced
- Salt and pepper to taste

For the Lettuce Wraps:

- 1 head iceberg lettuce or butter lettuce, leaves separated
- Thinly sliced cucumber, for serving
- Thinly sliced red onion, for serving
- Lime wedges, for serving

Instructions:

1. Cook the Chicken Larb:
   - Heat vegetable oil in a skillet over medium-high heat. Add shallots, garlic, and Thai chilies. Sauté until fragrant, about 1-2 minutes.
   - Add the ground chicken to the skillet. Cook until the chicken is browned and cooked through, breaking it up with a spoon, about 5-7 minutes.
   - Stir in fish sauce, lime juice, soy sauce, and erythritol or monk fruit sweetener (if using). Cook for an additional 2-3 minutes.
   - Remove from heat and stir in chopped cilantro, chopped mint, and sliced green onions. Season with salt and pepper to taste.
2. Prepare the Lettuce Wraps:

- Wash and dry the lettuce leaves. Arrange them on a serving platter.
3. Assemble the Lettuce Wraps:
   - Spoon the chicken larb mixture into each lettuce cup.
   - Top with thinly sliced cucumber and red onion.
4. Serve:
   - Serve the low-carb Thai Chicken Larb Lettuce Wraps with lime wedges on the side for squeezing over the filling.

These low-carb Thai Chicken Larb Lettuce Wraps are a flavorful and satisfying dish that's perfect for a light and healthy meal. Enjoy the savory chicken larb with the crisp freshness of lettuce and crunchy vegetables!

Thai-inspired Asparagus Salad with Chili Lime Dressing

Ingredients:

For the Salad:

- 1 lb (450g) asparagus spears, tough ends trimmed
- 1 red bell pepper, thinly sliced
- 1/4 cup chopped fresh cilantro
- 1/4 cup chopped fresh mint
- 2 green onions, thinly sliced
- 2 tablespoons chopped roasted peanuts or cashews (optional, for garnish)

For the Chili Lime Dressing:

- 3 tablespoons lime juice
- 2 tablespoons fish sauce
- 1 tablespoon soy sauce or tamari (for gluten-free option)
- 1 tablespoon honey or maple syrup
- 1 tablespoon vegetable oil
- 1-2 Thai bird's eye chilies, finely chopped (adjust to taste)
- 2 cloves garlic, minced
- 1 teaspoon grated ginger

Instructions:

1. Blanch the Asparagus:
   - Bring a large pot of salted water to a boil. Add the trimmed asparagus spears and blanch for 2-3 minutes, until just tender but still crisp. Remove the asparagus from the boiling water and immediately transfer to a bowl of ice water to stop the cooking process. Drain and pat dry with paper towels.
2. Prepare the Salad:
   - Cut the blanched asparagus spears into bite-sized pieces and place them in a large mixing bowl.
   - Add the thinly sliced red bell pepper, chopped cilantro, chopped mint, and sliced green onions to the bowl with the asparagus.
3. Make the Chili Lime Dressing:

- In a small bowl, whisk together lime juice, fish sauce, soy sauce, honey or maple syrup, vegetable oil, chopped Thai bird's eye chilies, minced garlic, and grated ginger until well combined.
4. Toss with Dressing:
   - Pour the chili lime dressing over the salad ingredients in the mixing bowl. Toss gently to coat everything evenly with the dressing.
5. Garnish and Serve:
   - Transfer the Thai-inspired Asparagus Salad with Chili Lime Dressing to a serving platter or individual plates.
   - If desired, garnish with chopped roasted peanuts or cashews for added crunch and flavor.

This Thai-inspired Asparagus Salad with Chili Lime Dressing is a vibrant and flavorful dish that's perfect as a side dish or light meal. Enjoy the crisp asparagus spears with the zesty, spicy dressing!

Low-carb Thai Spicy Pork Salad with Herbs

Ingredients:

For the Spicy Pork:

- 1 lb (450g) ground pork
- 2 tablespoons vegetable oil
- 3 shallots, finely chopped
- 3 cloves garlic, minced
- 1-2 Thai bird's eye chilies, finely chopped (adjust to taste)
- 2 tablespoons fish sauce
- 2 tablespoons lime juice
- 1 tablespoon soy sauce or tamari (for gluten-free option)
- 1 teaspoon erythritol or monk fruit sweetener (optional)
- Salt and pepper to taste

For the Salad:

- 4 cups mixed salad greens (such as lettuce, spinach, or arugula)
- 1 cucumber, thinly sliced
- 1 carrot, julienned or grated
- 1/2 red bell pepper, thinly sliced
- 1/2 yellow bell pepper, thinly sliced
- 1/4 cup fresh cilantro leaves, chopped
- 1/4 cup fresh mint leaves, chopped
- 2 green onions, thinly sliced

For the Dressing:

- 3 tablespoons lime juice
- 2 tablespoons fish sauce
- 1 tablespoon soy sauce or tamari
- 1 tablespoon sesame oil
- 1 tablespoon erythritol or monk fruit sweetener (optional)
- 1 Thai bird's eye chili, finely chopped (adjust to taste)
- 2 cloves garlic, minced
- 1 teaspoon grated ginger

Instructions:

1. Cook the Spicy Pork:
   - Heat vegetable oil in a skillet over medium-high heat. Add shallots, garlic, and Thai chilies. Sauté until fragrant, about 1-2 minutes.
   - Add the ground pork to the skillet. Cook until the pork is browned and cooked through, breaking it up with a spoon, about 5-7 minutes.
   - Stir in fish sauce, lime juice, soy sauce, and erythritol or monk fruit sweetener (if using). Cook for an additional 2-3 minutes.
   - Remove from heat and let cool slightly.
2. Prepare the Salad Ingredients:
   - In a large mixing bowl, combine the mixed salad greens, thinly sliced cucumber, julienned or grated carrot, thinly sliced red and yellow bell peppers, chopped cilantro, chopped mint, and sliced green onions. Toss gently to combine.
3. Make the Dressing:
   - In a small bowl, whisk together lime juice, fish sauce, soy sauce, sesame oil, erythritol or monk fruit sweetener (if using), chopped Thai bird's eye chili, minced garlic, and grated ginger until well combined.
4. Assemble the Salad:
   - Add the cooked spicy pork to the salad mixture in the large mixing bowl.
5. Toss with Dressing:
   - Pour the dressing over the salad ingredients. Toss gently until everything is evenly coated with the dressing.
6. Serve:
   - Divide the Low-carb Thai Spicy Pork Salad with Herbs among serving plates.
   - Enjoy immediately as a delicious and flavorful meal.

This Low-carb Thai Spicy Pork Salad with Herbs is a satisfying and vibrant dish that's perfect for a light and healthy meal. Enjoy the savory pork with the crisp freshness of the salad greens and herbs!

Thai-style Grilled Mushroom Salad with Soy Ginger Dressing

Ingredients:

For the Grilled Mushroom Salad:

- 1 lb (450g) mixed mushrooms (such as button mushrooms, shiitake mushrooms, and oyster mushrooms), cleaned and sliced if large
- 2 tablespoons vegetable oil
- Salt and pepper to taste
- 4 cups mixed salad greens (such as lettuce, spinach, or arugula)
- 1 cucumber, thinly sliced
- 1 carrot, julienned or grated
- 1/4 cup fresh cilantro leaves, chopped
- 1/4 cup fresh mint leaves, chopped
- 2 green onions, thinly sliced
- 2 tablespoons chopped roasted peanuts or cashews (optional, for garnish)

For the Soy Ginger Dressing:

- 3 tablespoons soy sauce or tamari
- 2 tablespoons rice vinegar
- 1 tablespoon sesame oil
- 1 tablespoon honey or maple syrup
- 1 tablespoon grated ginger
- 2 cloves garlic, minced
- 1 Thai bird's eye chili, finely chopped (optional, for added heat)
- 2 tablespoons vegetable oil

Instructions:

1. Grill the Mushrooms:
    - Preheat the grill to medium-high heat. Brush the sliced mushrooms with vegetable oil and season with salt and pepper.
    - Grill the mushrooms for 4-5 minutes per side, or until tender and lightly charred. Remove from the grill and let cool slightly.
2. Prepare the Salad Ingredients:

- In a large mixing bowl, combine the mixed salad greens, thinly sliced cucumber, julienned or grated carrot, chopped cilantro, chopped mint, and sliced green onions.
3. Make the Soy Ginger Dressing:
   - In a small bowl, whisk together soy sauce or tamari, rice vinegar, sesame oil, honey or maple syrup, grated ginger, minced garlic, and chopped Thai bird's eye chili (if using). Gradually whisk in vegetable oil until emulsified.
4. Assemble the Salad:
   - Add the grilled mushrooms to the salad mixture in the large mixing bowl.
5. Toss with Dressing:
   - Pour the soy ginger dressing over the salad ingredients. Toss gently until everything is evenly coated with the dressing.
6. Garnish and Serve:
   - Divide the Thai-style Grilled Mushroom Salad with Soy Ginger Dressing among serving plates.
   - If desired, garnish with chopped roasted peanuts or cashews for added crunch and flavor.

This Thai-style Grilled Mushroom Salad with Soy Ginger Dressing is a delicious and satisfying dish that's perfect as a light and flavorful meal. Enjoy the smoky grilled mushrooms with the zesty, savory dressing!

Low-carb Thai Shrimp Larb Salad with Mint

Ingredients:

For the Shrimp Larb:

- 1 lb (450g) shrimp, peeled and deveined
- 2 tablespoons vegetable oil
- 3 shallots, finely chopped
- 3 cloves garlic, minced
- 1-2 Thai bird's eye chilies, finely chopped (adjust to taste)
- 2 tablespoons fish sauce
- 2 tablespoons lime juice
- 1 tablespoon soy sauce or tamari (for gluten-free option)
- 1 teaspoon erythritol or monk fruit sweetener (optional)
- Salt and pepper to taste

For the Salad:

- 4 cups mixed salad greens (such as lettuce, spinach, or arugula)
- 1 cucumber, thinly sliced
- 1 carrot, julienned or grated
- 1/2 red bell pepper, thinly sliced
- 1/2 yellow bell pepper, thinly sliced
- 1/4 cup fresh mint leaves, chopped
- 2 green onions, thinly sliced
- 2 tablespoons chopped roasted peanuts or cashews (optional, for garnish)

For the Dressing:

- 3 tablespoons lime juice
- 2 tablespoons fish sauce
- 1 tablespoon soy sauce or tamari
- 1 tablespoon sesame oil
- 1 tablespoon erythritol or monk fruit sweetener (optional)
- 1 Thai bird's eye chili, finely chopped (adjust to taste)
- 2 cloves garlic, minced
- 1 teaspoon grated ginger

Instructions:

1. Prepare the Shrimp Larb:
   - Heat vegetable oil in a skillet over medium-high heat. Add shallots, garlic, and Thai chilies. Sauté until fragrant, about 1-2 minutes.
   - Add the shrimp to the skillet. Cook until the shrimp are pink and cooked through, about 2-3 minutes.
   - Stir in fish sauce, lime juice, soy sauce, and erythritol or monk fruit sweetener (if using). Cook for an additional 1-2 minutes.
   - Remove from heat and let cool slightly.
2. Prepare the Salad Ingredients:
   - In a large mixing bowl, combine the mixed salad greens, thinly sliced cucumber, julienned or grated carrot, thinly sliced red and yellow bell peppers, chopped mint leaves, and sliced green onions.
3. Make the Dressing:
   - In a small bowl, whisk together lime juice, fish sauce, soy sauce, sesame oil, erythritol or monk fruit sweetener (if using), chopped Thai bird's eye chili, minced garlic, and grated ginger until well combined.
4. Assemble the Salad:
   - Add the cooked shrimp larb to the salad mixture in the large mixing bowl.
5. Toss with Dressing:
   - Pour the dressing over the salad ingredients. Toss gently until everything is evenly coated with the dressing.
6. Garnish and Serve:
   - Divide the Low-carb Thai Shrimp Larb Salad with Mint among serving plates.
   - If desired, garnish with chopped roasted peanuts or cashews for added crunch and flavor.

This Low-carb Thai Shrimp Larb Salad with Mint is a light and flavorful dish that's perfect for a healthy and satisfying meal. Enjoy the succulent shrimp with the crisp freshness of the salad greens and aromatic mint!

Thai-inspired Radish Salad with Lime Dressing

Ingredients:

For the Radish Salad:

- 1 bunch radishes, thinly sliced
- 1/2 cucumber, thinly sliced
- 1/4 cup chopped fresh cilantro
- 2 tablespoons chopped fresh mint
- 2 green onions, thinly sliced
- 2 tablespoons chopped roasted peanuts or cashews (optional, for garnish)

For the Lime Dressing:

- 3 tablespoons lime juice
- 2 tablespoons fish sauce
- 1 tablespoon soy sauce or tamari (for gluten-free option)
- 1 tablespoon sesame oil
- 1 tablespoon honey or maple syrup
- 1 Thai bird's eye chili, finely chopped (adjust to taste)
- 2 cloves garlic, minced
- 1 teaspoon grated ginger

Instructions:

1. Prepare the Radish Salad:
   - In a large mixing bowl, combine the thinly sliced radishes, thinly sliced cucumber, chopped cilantro, chopped mint, and sliced green onions.
2. Make the Lime Dressing:
   - In a small bowl, whisk together lime juice, fish sauce, soy sauce, sesame oil, honey or maple syrup, chopped Thai bird's eye chili, minced garlic, and grated ginger until well combined.
3. Toss with Dressing:
   - Pour the lime dressing over the radish salad ingredients. Toss gently until everything is evenly coated with the dressing.
4. Garnish and Serve:
   - Divide the Thai-inspired Radish Salad with Lime Dressing among serving plates.

- If desired, garnish with chopped roasted peanuts or cashews for added crunch and flavor.

This Thai-inspired Radish Salad with Lime Dressing is a vibrant and refreshing dish that's perfect as a side dish or light meal. Enjoy the crispness of the radishes and cucumber with the tangy and aromatic dressing!

Low-carb Thai Chicken Satay Zoodle Salad

Ingredients:

For the Chicken Satay:

- 1 lb (450g) chicken breast, cut into thin strips
- 2 tablespoons soy sauce or tamari (for gluten-free option)
- 2 tablespoons coconut milk
- 1 tablespoon fish sauce
- 1 tablespoon lime juice
- 1 tablespoon honey or maple syrup
- 1 teaspoon grated ginger
- 2 cloves garlic, minced
- 1 teaspoon curry powder
- Bamboo skewers, soaked in water for 30 minutes

For the Zoodle Salad:

- 2 medium zucchinis, spiralized into noodles
- 1 carrot, spiralized into noodles or julienned
- 1/2 red bell pepper, thinly sliced
- 1/2 yellow bell pepper, thinly sliced
- 1/4 cup chopped fresh cilantro
- 1/4 cup chopped roasted peanuts (optional, for garnish)

For the Peanut Dressing:

- 1/4 cup creamy peanut butter
- 2 tablespoons coconut milk
- 2 tablespoons soy sauce or tamari
- 1 tablespoon lime juice
- 1 tablespoon fish sauce
- 1 tablespoon honey or maple syrup
- 1 teaspoon grated ginger
- 1 clove garlic, minced
- 1 Thai bird's eye chili, finely chopped (optional, for added heat)
- Water, as needed to thin the dressing

Instructions:

1. Marinate the Chicken Satay:
   - In a bowl, whisk together soy sauce or tamari, coconut milk, fish sauce, lime juice, honey or maple syrup, grated ginger, minced garlic, and curry powder to make the marinade.
   - Add the chicken strips to the marinade, turning to coat evenly. Cover and refrigerate for at least 30 minutes or up to 4 hours.
2. Prepare the Peanut Dressing:
   - In a small bowl, whisk together peanut butter, coconut milk, soy sauce or tamari, lime juice, fish sauce, honey or maple syrup, grated ginger, minced garlic, and chopped Thai bird's eye chili (if using) until smooth. If the dressing is too thick, add water, a tablespoon at a time, until desired consistency is reached. Set aside.
3. Grill the Chicken Satay:
   - Preheat a grill or grill pan over medium-high heat. Thread the marinated chicken strips onto soaked bamboo skewers.
   - Grill the chicken satay for 3-4 minutes per side, or until cooked through and slightly charred. Remove from the grill and set aside.
4. Assemble the Zoodle Salad:
   - In a large mixing bowl, combine the zucchini noodles, carrot noodles, sliced red and yellow bell peppers, and chopped cilantro.
5. Toss with Dressing:
   - Pour the peanut dressing over the zoodle salad ingredients. Toss gently until everything is evenly coated with the dressing.
6. Serve:
   - Divide the Low-carb Thai Chicken Satay Zoodle Salad among serving plates.
   - Top with grilled chicken satay skewers.
   - If desired, garnish with chopped roasted peanuts.

This Low-carb Thai Chicken Satay Zoodle Salad is a light and flavorful dish that's perfect for a healthy and satisfying meal. Enjoy the tender grilled chicken satay with the crisp freshness of zucchini noodles and the creamy peanut dressing!

Thai-style Spicy Beef Larb Lettuce Wraps

Ingredients:

For the Spicy Beef Larb:

- 1 lb (450g) ground beef
- 2 tablespoons vegetable oil
- 3 shallots, finely chopped
- 3 cloves garlic, minced
- 1-2 Thai bird's eye chilies, finely chopped (adjust to taste)
- 2 tablespoons fish sauce
- 2 tablespoons lime juice
- 1 tablespoon soy sauce or tamari (for gluten-free option)
- 1 teaspoon erythritol or monk fruit sweetener (optional)
- Salt and pepper to taste

For the Lettuce Wraps:

- 1 head iceberg lettuce or butter lettuce, leaves separated
- Thinly sliced cucumber, for serving
- Thinly sliced red onion, for serving
- Lime wedges, for serving

Optional Garnish:

- Chopped fresh cilantro
- Chopped fresh mint
- Chopped roasted peanuts or cashews

Instructions:

1. Cook the Spicy Beef Larb:
   - Heat vegetable oil in a skillet over medium-high heat. Add shallots, garlic, and Thai chilies. Sauté until fragrant, about 1-2 minutes.
   - Add the ground beef to the skillet. Cook until the beef is browned and cooked through, breaking it up with a spoon, about 5-7 minutes.
   - Stir in fish sauce, lime juice, soy sauce, and erythritol or monk fruit sweetener (if using). Cook for an additional 2-3 minutes.
   - Remove from heat and let cool slightly.

2. Prepare the Lettuce Wraps:
   - Wash and dry the lettuce leaves. Arrange them on a serving platter.
3. Assemble the Lettuce Wraps:
   - Spoon the spicy beef larb mixture into each lettuce cup.
   - Top with thinly sliced cucumber and red onion.
4. Serve:
   - Serve the Thai-style Spicy Beef Larb Lettuce Wraps with lime wedges on the side for squeezing over the filling.
   - Optionally, garnish with chopped fresh cilantro, chopped fresh mint, and chopped roasted peanuts or cashews.

Enjoy these Thai-style Spicy Beef Larb Lettuce Wraps as a flavorful and satisfying appetizer or light meal. The combination of savory beef larb and crisp lettuce leaves makes for a delicious and refreshing dish!

Low-carb Thai Turkey Larb Salad with Cucumber

Ingredients:

For the Turkey Larb:

- 1 lb (450g) ground turkey
- 2 tablespoons vegetable oil
- 3 shallots, finely chopped
- 3 cloves garlic, minced
- 1-2 Thai bird's eye chilies, finely chopped (adjust to taste)
- 2 tablespoons fish sauce
- 2 tablespoons lime juice
- 1 tablespoon soy sauce or tamari (for gluten-free option)
- 1 teaspoon erythritol or monk fruit sweetener (optional)
- Salt and pepper to taste

For the Salad:

- 1 large cucumber, thinly sliced
- 1/4 cup chopped fresh cilantro
- 1/4 cup chopped fresh mint
- 2 green onions, thinly sliced
- 2 tablespoons chopped roasted peanuts or cashews (optional, for garnish)

For Serving:

- Lettuce leaves or cabbage leaves, for wrapping
- Lime wedges

Instructions:

1. Cook the Turkey Larb:
   - Heat vegetable oil in a skillet over medium-high heat. Add shallots, garlic, and Thai chilies. Sauté until fragrant, about 1-2 minutes.
   - Add the ground turkey to the skillet. Cook until the turkey is browned and cooked through, breaking it up with a spoon, about 5-7 minutes.
   - Stir in fish sauce, lime juice, soy sauce, and erythritol or monk fruit sweetener (if using). Cook for an additional 2-3 minutes.
   - Remove from heat and let cool slightly.

2. Prepare the Salad Ingredients:
   - In a large mixing bowl, combine the thinly sliced cucumber, chopped cilantro, chopped mint, and sliced green onions.
3. Assemble the Salad:
   - Add the cooked turkey larb to the salad mixture in the large mixing bowl. Toss gently to combine.
4. Serve:
   - Serve the Low-carb Thai Turkey Larb Salad with Cucumber with lettuce leaves or cabbage leaves for wrapping.
   - Optionally, garnish with chopped roasted peanuts or cashews.
   - Serve with lime wedges on the side for squeezing over the salad.

Enjoy this Low-carb Thai Turkey Larb Salad with Cucumber as a light and flavorful meal. The combination of seasoned ground turkey and crisp cucumber makes for a delicious and refreshing dish!

Thai-inspired Brussels Sprouts Salad with Sesame Dressing

Ingredients:

For the Brussels Sprouts Salad:

- 1 lb (450g) Brussels sprouts, trimmed and thinly sliced or shredded
- 1 carrot, grated or julienned
- 1/2 red bell pepper, thinly sliced
- 1/2 yellow bell pepper, thinly sliced
- 1/4 cup chopped fresh cilantro
- 1/4 cup chopped fresh mint
- 2 green onions, thinly sliced
- 2 tablespoons toasted sesame seeds (optional, for garnish)

For the Sesame Dressing:

- 3 tablespoons rice vinegar
- 2 tablespoons soy sauce or tamari
- 1 tablespoon sesame oil
- 1 tablespoon honey or maple syrup
- 1 tablespoon grated ginger
- 2 cloves garlic, minced
- 1 teaspoon chili garlic sauce or Sriracha (adjust to taste)
- Salt and pepper to taste

Instructions:

1. Prepare the Brussels Sprouts Salad:
   - In a large mixing bowl, combine the thinly sliced or shredded Brussels sprouts, grated or julienned carrot, thinly sliced red and yellow bell peppers, chopped cilantro, chopped mint, and sliced green onions.
2. Make the Sesame Dressing:
   - In a small bowl, whisk together rice vinegar, soy sauce or tamari, sesame oil, honey or maple syrup, grated ginger, minced garlic, chili garlic sauce or Sriracha, salt, and pepper until well combined.
3. Toss with Dressing:
   - Pour the sesame dressing over the Brussels sprouts salad ingredients. Toss gently until everything is evenly coated with the dressing.

4. Garnish and Serve:
   - Transfer the Thai-inspired Brussels Sprouts Salad with Sesame Dressing to a serving platter or individual plates.
   - If desired, garnish with toasted sesame seeds for added flavor and texture.

This Thai-inspired Brussels Sprouts Salad with Sesame Dressing is a vibrant and flavorful dish that's perfect as a side dish or light meal. Enjoy the crispness of the Brussels sprouts and the nuttiness of the sesame dressing!

Low-carb Thai Tofu Larb Salad with Lime

Ingredients:

For the Tofu Larb:

- 1 block (14 oz / 400g) extra-firm tofu, pressed and crumbled
- 2 tablespoons vegetable oil
- 3 shallots, finely chopped
- 3 cloves garlic, minced
- 1-2 Thai bird's eye chilies, finely chopped (adjust to taste)
- 2 tablespoons fish sauce
- 2 tablespoons lime juice
- 1 tablespoon soy sauce or tamari (for gluten-free option)
- 1 teaspoon erythritol or monk fruit sweetener (optional)
- Salt and pepper to taste

For the Salad:

- 4 cups mixed salad greens (such as lettuce, spinach, or arugula)
- 1 cucumber, thinly sliced
- 1 carrot, julienned or grated
- 1/4 cup chopped fresh cilantro
- 1/4 cup chopped fresh mint
- 2 green onions, thinly sliced

For Serving:

- Lime wedges

Instructions:

1. Prepare the Tofu Larb:
   - Heat vegetable oil in a skillet over medium-high heat. Add shallots, garlic, and Thai chilies. Sauté until fragrant, about 1-2 minutes.
   - Add the crumbled tofu to the skillet. Cook until the tofu is lightly browned and heated through, about 5-7 minutes.
   - Stir in fish sauce, lime juice, soy sauce, and erythritol or monk fruit sweetener (if using). Cook for an additional 2-3 minutes.
   - Remove from heat and let cool slightly.

2. Prepare the Salad Ingredients:
   - In a large mixing bowl, combine the mixed salad greens, thinly sliced cucumber, julienned or grated carrot, chopped cilantro, chopped mint, and sliced green onions.
3. Assemble the Salad:
   - Add the cooked tofu larb to the salad mixture in the large mixing bowl. Toss gently to combine.
4. Serve:
   - Divide the Low-carb Thai Tofu Larb Salad with Lime among serving plates.
   - Serve with lime wedges on the side for squeezing over the salad.

Enjoy this Low-carb Thai Tofu Larb Salad with Lime as a light and flavorful meal. The combination of seasoned tofu and fresh salad greens, herbs, and vegetables makes for a delicious and satisfying dish!

Thai-style Grilled Salmon Salad with Coconut Dressing

Ingredients:

For the Grilled Salmon:

- 4 salmon fillets (6 oz / 170g each)
- 2 tablespoons soy sauce or tamari
- 2 tablespoons lime juice
- 1 tablespoon fish sauce
- 1 tablespoon honey or maple syrup
- 2 cloves garlic, minced
- 1 teaspoon grated ginger
- 1 teaspoon sesame oil
- Salt and pepper to taste

For the Coconut Dressing:

- 1/2 cup canned coconut milk
- 2 tablespoons lime juice
- 1 tablespoon fish sauce
- 1 tablespoon soy sauce or tamari
- 1 tablespoon honey or maple syrup
- 1 teaspoon grated ginger
- 1 clove garlic, minced
- 1 Thai bird's eye chili, finely chopped (optional, for added heat)

For the Salad:

- 4 cups mixed salad greens (such as lettuce, spinach, or arugula)
- 1 cucumber, thinly sliced
- 1 carrot, julienned or grated
- 1/2 red bell pepper, thinly sliced
- 1/2 yellow bell pepper, thinly sliced
- 1/4 cup chopped fresh cilantro
- 1/4 cup chopped fresh mint
- 2 green onions, thinly sliced
- 1/4 cup chopped roasted peanuts or cashews (optional, for garnish)

Instructions:

1. Marinate the Salmon:
   - In a shallow dish, whisk together soy sauce or tamari, lime juice, fish sauce, honey or maple syrup, minced garlic, grated ginger, sesame oil, salt, and pepper.
   - Add the salmon fillets to the marinade, turning to coat evenly. Cover and refrigerate for at least 30 minutes, or up to 2 hours.
2. Prepare the Coconut Dressing:
   - In a small bowl, whisk together canned coconut milk, lime juice, fish sauce, soy sauce or tamari, honey or maple syrup, grated ginger, minced garlic, and chopped Thai bird's eye chili (if using). Set aside.
3. Grill the Salmon:
   - Preheat the grill to medium-high heat. Remove the salmon fillets from the marinade and discard the excess marinade.
   - Grill the salmon fillets for 4-5 minutes per side, or until cooked through and lightly charred. Remove from the grill and let cool slightly.
4. Assemble the Salad:
   - In a large mixing bowl, combine the mixed salad greens, thinly sliced cucumber, julienned or grated carrot, thinly sliced red and yellow bell peppers, chopped cilantro, chopped mint, and sliced green onions.
5. Assemble the Salad:
   - Divide the mixed salad greens among serving plates.
   - Top each salad plate with a grilled salmon fillet.
6. Drizzle with Coconut Dressing:
   - Drizzle the coconut dressing over the grilled salmon and salad greens.
7. Garnish and Serve:
   - Optionally, garnish each salad with chopped roasted peanuts or cashews.
   - Serve the Thai-style Grilled Salmon Salad with Coconut Dressing immediately.

Enjoy this Thai-inspired Grilled Salmon Salad with Coconut Dressing as a light and flavorful meal. The combination of grilled salmon and creamy coconut dressing with fresh salad greens and vegetables is simply irresistible!

Low-carb Thai Pork Larb Salad with Cabbage

Ingredients:

For the Pork Larb:

- 1 lb (450g) ground pork
- 2 tablespoons vegetable oil
- 3 shallots, finely chopped
- 3 cloves garlic, minced
- 1-2 Thai bird's eye chilies, finely chopped (adjust to taste)
- 2 tablespoons fish sauce
- 2 tablespoons lime juice
- 1 tablespoon soy sauce or tamari (for gluten-free option)
- 1 teaspoon erythritol or monk fruit sweetener (optional)
- Salt and pepper to taste

For the Cabbage:

- 1 head of cabbage, leaves separated

For the Salad:

- 1 cucumber, thinly sliced
- 1 carrot, julienned or grated
- 1/4 cup chopped fresh cilantro
- 1/4 cup chopped fresh mint
- 2 green onions, thinly sliced

Instructions:

1. Cook the Pork Larb:
   - Heat vegetable oil in a skillet over medium-high heat. Add shallots, garlic, and Thai chilies. Sauté until fragrant, about 1-2 minutes.
   - Add the ground pork to the skillet. Cook until the pork is browned and cooked through, breaking it up with a spoon, about 5-7 minutes.
   - Stir in fish sauce, lime juice, soy sauce, and erythritol or monk fruit sweetener (if using). Cook for an additional 2-3 minutes.
   - Remove from heat and let cool slightly.
2. Prepare the Cabbage Leaves:

- Wash and dry the cabbage leaves. Arrange them on a serving platter.
3. Prepare the Salad Ingredients:
   - In a large mixing bowl, combine the thinly sliced cucumber, julienned or grated carrot, chopped cilantro, chopped mint, and sliced green onions.
4. Assemble the Salad:
   - Spoon the cooked pork larb onto the cabbage leaves.
5. Serve:
   - Serve the Low-carb Thai Pork Larb Salad with Cabbage alongside the prepared salad mixture.
   - Optionally, garnish the salad with additional fresh herbs and lime wedges.

Enjoy this Low-carb Thai Pork Larb Salad with Cabbage as a flavorful and satisfying meal. The combination of seasoned ground pork and crisp cabbage leaves is a delightful way to enjoy Thai flavors!

Thai-inspired Green Bean Salad with Peanut Dressing

Ingredients:

For the Green Bean Salad:

- 1 lb (450g) green beans, trimmed
- 1 red bell pepper, thinly sliced
- 1/4 cup chopped fresh cilantro
- 1/4 cup chopped fresh mint
- 2 green onions, thinly sliced
- 1/4 cup chopped roasted peanuts (optional, for garnish)

For the Peanut Dressing:

- 1/4 cup creamy peanut butter
- 2 tablespoons rice vinegar
- 2 tablespoons soy sauce or tamari
- 1 tablespoon sesame oil
- 1 tablespoon honey or maple syrup
- 1 teaspoon grated ginger
- 1 clove garlic, minced
- 1 Thai bird's eye chili, finely chopped (optional, for added heat)
- Water, as needed to thin the dressing

Instructions:

1. Blanch the Green Beans:
    - Bring a pot of salted water to a boil. Add the green beans and cook for 2-3 minutes, or until crisp-tender. Drain the green beans and immediately transfer them to a bowl of ice water to stop the cooking process. Once cooled, drain and pat dry with paper towels.
2. Prepare the Peanut Dressing:
    - In a small bowl, whisk together peanut butter, rice vinegar, soy sauce or tamari, sesame oil, honey or maple syrup, grated ginger, minced garlic, and chopped Thai bird's eye chili (if using). If the dressing is too thick, add water, a tablespoon at a time, until desired consistency is reached. Set aside.
3. Assemble the Salad:

- In a large mixing bowl, combine the blanched green beans, thinly sliced red bell pepper, chopped cilantro, chopped mint, and sliced green onions.
4. Toss with Dressing:
   - Pour the peanut dressing over the salad ingredients. Toss gently until everything is evenly coated with the dressing.
5. Garnish and Serve:
   - Transfer the Thai-inspired Green Bean Salad with Peanut Dressing to a serving platter or individual plates.
   - If desired, garnish with chopped roasted peanuts for added crunch and flavor.

Enjoy this Thai-inspired Green Bean Salad with Peanut Dressing as a refreshing side dish or light meal. The combination of crisp green beans and zesty peanut dressing is sure to tantalize your taste buds!

Low-carb Thai Chicken Larb Salad with Bell Peppers

Ingredients:

For the Chicken Larb:

- 1 lb (450g) ground chicken
- 2 tablespoons vegetable oil
- 3 shallots, finely chopped
- 3 cloves garlic, minced
- 1-2 Thai bird's eye chilies, finely chopped (adjust to taste)
- 2 tablespoons fish sauce
- 2 tablespoons lime juice
- 1 tablespoon soy sauce or tamari (for gluten-free option)
- 1 teaspoon erythritol or monk fruit sweetener (optional)
- Salt and pepper to taste

For the Salad:

- 2 bell peppers (red, yellow, or orange), thinly sliced
- 4 cups mixed salad greens (such as lettuce, spinach, or arugula)
- 1/4 cup chopped fresh cilantro
- 1/4 cup chopped fresh mint
- 2 green onions, thinly sliced
- 1/4 cup chopped roasted peanuts or cashews (optional, for garnish)

Instructions:

1. Cook the Chicken Larb:
   - Heat vegetable oil in a skillet over medium-high heat. Add shallots, garlic, and Thai chilies. Sauté until fragrant, about 1-2 minutes.
   - Add the ground chicken to the skillet. Cook until the chicken is browned and cooked through, breaking it up with a spoon, about 5-7 minutes.
   - Stir in fish sauce, lime juice, soy sauce, and erythritol or monk fruit sweetener (if using). Cook for an additional 2-3 minutes.
   - Remove from heat and let cool slightly.
2. Prepare the Salad Ingredients:
   - In a large mixing bowl, combine the thinly sliced bell peppers, mixed salad greens, chopped cilantro, chopped mint, and sliced green onions.

3. Assemble the Salad:
   - Add the cooked chicken larb to the salad mixture in the large mixing bowl. Toss gently to combine.
4. Serve:
   - Divide the Low-carb Thai Chicken Larb Salad with Bell Peppers among serving plates.
   - If desired, garnish with chopped roasted peanuts or cashews for added crunch and flavor.

Enjoy this Low-carb Thai Chicken Larb Salad with Bell Peppers as a light and satisfying meal. The combination of seasoned ground chicken, crisp bell peppers, and fresh herbs makes for a delicious and nutritious dish!

Thai-style Spicy Beef Salad with Basil

Ingredients:

For the Beef Salad:

- 1 lb (450g) beef steak (such as sirloin or flank), thinly sliced
- 2 tablespoons vegetable oil
- 3 shallots, thinly sliced
- 3 cloves garlic, minced
- 1-2 Thai bird's eye chilies, finely chopped (adjust to taste)
- 2 tablespoons fish sauce
- 2 tablespoons lime juice
- 1 tablespoon soy sauce or tamari (for gluten-free option)
- 1 teaspoon erythritol or monk fruit sweetener (optional)
- Salt and pepper to taste
- 1 cup fresh basil leaves, torn

For Serving:

- Mixed salad greens
- Lime wedges
- Additional fresh basil leaves for garnish
- Chopped roasted peanuts (optional)

Instructions:

1. Marinate the Beef:
   - In a bowl, combine the sliced beef with fish sauce, lime juice, soy sauce or tamari, erythritol or monk fruit sweetener (if using), salt, and pepper. Let it marinate for at least 30 minutes in the refrigerator.
2. Cook the Beef:
   - Heat vegetable oil in a skillet over medium-high heat. Add shallots, garlic, and Thai chilies. Sauté until fragrant, about 1-2 minutes.
   - Add the marinated beef to the skillet. Cook until the beef is browned and cooked to your desired doneness, about 3-4 minutes for medium-rare.
   - Remove from heat and let cool slightly.
3. Assemble the Salad:

- In a large mixing bowl, combine the cooked beef mixture with torn basil leaves. Toss gently to combine.
4. Serve:
    - Arrange mixed salad greens on serving plates.
    - Top the salad greens with the Thai-style spicy beef and basil mixture.
    - Garnish with additional fresh basil leaves and chopped roasted peanuts (if using).
    - Serve with lime wedges on the side for squeezing over the salad.

Enjoy this Thai-style Spicy Beef Salad with Basil as a flavorful and satisfying meal. The combination of tender beef, aromatic basil, and zesty dressing is sure to delight your taste buds!

Low-carb Thai Shrimp Larb Salad with Cilantro

Ingredients:

For the Shrimp Larb:

- 1 lb (450g) shrimp, peeled and deveined
- 2 tablespoons vegetable oil
- 3 shallots, finely chopped
- 3 cloves garlic, minced
- 1-2 Thai bird's eye chilies, finely chopped (adjust to taste)
- 2 tablespoons fish sauce
- 2 tablespoons lime juice
- 1 tablespoon soy sauce or tamari (for gluten-free option)
- 1 teaspoon erythritol or monk fruit sweetener (optional)
- Salt and pepper to taste

For the Salad:

- 4 cups mixed salad greens (such as lettuce, spinach, or arugula)
- 1/2 cup chopped fresh cilantro
- 1/4 cup chopped fresh mint
- 2 green onions, thinly sliced
- 1/4 cup chopped roasted peanuts or cashews (optional, for garnish)

Instructions:

1. Cook the Shrimp Larb:
   - Heat vegetable oil in a skillet over medium-high heat. Add shallots, garlic, and Thai chilies. Sauté until fragrant, about 1-2 minutes.
   - Add the shrimp to the skillet. Cook until the shrimp is pink and cooked through, about 2-3 minutes per side.
   - Stir in fish sauce, lime juice, soy sauce, and erythritol or monk fruit sweetener (if using). Cook for an additional 2-3 minutes.
   - Remove from heat and let cool slightly.
2. Prepare the Salad Ingredients:
   - In a large mixing bowl, combine the mixed salad greens, chopped cilantro, chopped mint, and sliced green onions.
3. Assemble the Salad:

- Add the cooked shrimp larb to the salad mixture in the large mixing bowl. Toss gently to combine.
4. Serve:
    - Divide the Low-carb Thai Shrimp Larb Salad with Cilantro among serving plates.
    - If desired, garnish with chopped roasted peanuts or cashews for added crunch and flavor.

Enjoy this Low-carb Thai Shrimp Larb Salad with Cilantro as a light and flavorful meal. The combination of seasoned shrimp, fresh herbs, and zesty dressing is sure to please your palate!

Thai-inspired Cabbage Salad with Fish Sauce Dressing

Ingredients:

For the Salad:

- 1/2 head of cabbage, thinly sliced
- 1 carrot, julienned or grated
- 1/2 red bell pepper, thinly sliced
- 1/2 yellow bell pepper, thinly sliced
- 1/4 cup chopped fresh cilantro
- 1/4 cup chopped fresh mint
- 2 green onions, thinly sliced

For the Fish Sauce Dressing:

- 3 tablespoons fish sauce
- 2 tablespoons lime juice
- 1 tablespoon rice vinegar
- 1 tablespoon soy sauce or tamari
- 1 tablespoon honey or maple syrup
- 1 teaspoon grated ginger
- 1 clove garlic, minced
- 1 Thai bird's eye chili, finely chopped (optional, for added heat)

Optional Garnish:

- Chopped roasted peanuts or cashews
- Thinly sliced red chili

Instructions:

1. Prepare the Salad Ingredients:
   - In a large mixing bowl, combine the thinly sliced cabbage, julienned or grated carrot, thinly sliced red and yellow bell peppers, chopped cilantro, chopped mint, and sliced green onions.
2. Make the Fish Sauce Dressing:
   - In a small bowl, whisk together fish sauce, lime juice, rice vinegar, soy sauce or tamari, honey or maple syrup, grated ginger, minced garlic, and chopped Thai bird's eye chili (if using). Set aside.

3. Assemble the Salad:
   - Pour the fish sauce dressing over the salad ingredients in the large mixing bowl. Toss gently until everything is evenly coated with the dressing.
4. Garnish and Serve:
   - Optionally, garnish the Thai-inspired Cabbage Salad with Fish Sauce Dressing with chopped roasted peanuts or cashews and thinly sliced red chili for added texture and heat.
5. Chill and Serve:
   - Let the salad chill in the refrigerator for about 15-30 minutes before serving to allow the flavors to meld.

Enjoy this Thai-inspired Cabbage Salad with Fish Sauce Dressing as a refreshing side dish or light meal. The combination of crisp cabbage, colorful vegetables, and zesty fish sauce dressing is sure to tantalize your taste buds!

Low-carb Thai Turkey Larb Salad with Mint

Ingredients:

For the Turkey Larb:

- 1 lb (450g) ground turkey
- 2 tablespoons vegetable oil
- 3 shallots, finely chopped
- 3 cloves garlic, minced
- 1-2 Thai bird's eye chilies, finely chopped (adjust to taste)
- 2 tablespoons fish sauce
- 2 tablespoons lime juice
- 1 tablespoon soy sauce or tamari (for gluten-free option)
- 1 teaspoon erythritol or monk fruit sweetener (optional)
- Salt and pepper to taste

For the Salad:

- 4 cups mixed salad greens (such as lettuce, spinach, or arugula)
- 1/2 cup chopped fresh mint leaves
- 1/4 cup chopped fresh cilantro
- 2 green onions, thinly sliced
- 1/4 cup chopped roasted peanuts or cashews (optional, for garnish)

Instructions:

1. Cook the Turkey Larb:
   - Heat vegetable oil in a skillet over medium-high heat. Add shallots, garlic, and Thai chilies. Sauté until fragrant, about 1-2 minutes.
   - Add the ground turkey to the skillet. Cook until the turkey is browned and cooked through, breaking it up with a spoon, about 5-7 minutes.
   - Stir in fish sauce, lime juice, soy sauce, and erythritol or monk fruit sweetener (if using). Cook for an additional 2-3 minutes.
   - Remove from heat and let cool slightly.
2. Prepare the Salad Ingredients:
   - In a large mixing bowl, combine the mixed salad greens, chopped mint leaves, chopped cilantro, and sliced green onions.
3. Assemble the Salad:

- Add the cooked turkey larb to the salad mixture in the large mixing bowl. Toss gently to combine.
4. Serve:
    - Divide the Low-carb Thai Turkey Larb Salad with Mint among serving plates.
    - If desired, garnish with chopped roasted peanuts or cashews for added crunch and flavor.

Enjoy this Low-carb Thai Turkey Larb Salad with Mint as a light and flavorful meal. The combination of seasoned ground turkey and aromatic mint leaves is sure to satisfy your taste buds!

Thai-style Grilled Squid Salad with Lime Dressing

Ingredients:

For the Grilled Squid:

- 1 lb (450g) whole squid, cleaned and scored
- 2 tablespoons vegetable oil
- Salt and pepper to taste

For the Lime Dressing:

- 3 tablespoons lime juice
- 2 tablespoons fish sauce
- 1 tablespoon soy sauce or tamari (for gluten-free option)
- 1 tablespoon honey or maple syrup
- 1 teaspoon grated ginger
- 1 clove garlic, minced
- 1 Thai bird's eye chili, finely chopped (optional, for added heat)

For the Salad:

- 4 cups mixed salad greens (such as lettuce, spinach, or arugula)
- 1 cucumber, thinly sliced
- 1 carrot, julienned or grated
- 1/4 cup chopped fresh cilantro
- 1/4 cup chopped fresh mint
- 2 green onions, thinly sliced

For Serving:

- Lime wedges
- Additional chopped cilantro and mint for garnish

Instructions:

1. Prepare the Squid:
    - Preheat grill to medium-high heat.
    - Brush the cleaned and scored squid with vegetable oil and season with salt and pepper.

- Grill the squid for 2-3 minutes per side, or until opaque and lightly charred. Remove from grill and let cool slightly.
2. Prepare the Lime Dressing:
   - In a small bowl, whisk together lime juice, fish sauce, soy sauce or tamari, honey or maple syrup, grated ginger, minced garlic, and chopped Thai bird's eye chili (if using). Set aside.
3. Assemble the Salad:
   - In a large mixing bowl, combine the mixed salad greens, thinly sliced cucumber, julienned or grated carrot, chopped cilantro, chopped mint, and sliced green onions.
4. Slice the Squid:
   - Slice the grilled squid into rings or pieces.
5. Assemble the Salad:
   - Add the sliced grilled squid to the salad mixture in the large mixing bowl.
6. Toss with Dressing:
   - Pour the lime dressing over the salad ingredients. Toss gently until everything is evenly coated with the dressing.
7. Serve:
   - Divide the Thai-style Grilled Squid Salad with Lime Dressing among serving plates.
   - Garnish with additional chopped cilantro and mint.
   - Serve with lime wedges on the side for squeezing over the salad.

Enjoy this Thai-style Grilled Squid Salad with Lime Dressing as a light and refreshing meal. The combination of tender grilled squid and zesty lime dressing is sure to impress!

Low-carb Thai Tofu Larb Salad with Lemongrass

Ingredients:

For the Tofu Larb:

- 1 block (14 oz / 400g) extra-firm tofu, pressed and crumbled
- 2 tablespoons vegetable oil
- 3 shallots, finely chopped
- 3 cloves garlic, minced
- 1-2 Thai bird's eye chilies, finely chopped (adjust to taste)
- 2 stalks lemongrass, white part only, finely chopped
- 2 tablespoons fish sauce
- 2 tablespoons lime juice
- 1 tablespoon soy sauce or tamari (for gluten-free option)
- 1 teaspoon erythritol or monk fruit sweetener (optional)
- Salt and pepper to taste

For the Salad:

- 4 cups mixed salad greens (such as lettuce, spinach, or arugula)
- 1 cucumber, thinly sliced
- 1 carrot, julienned or grated
- 1/4 cup chopped fresh cilantro
- 1/4 cup chopped fresh mint
- 2 green onions, thinly sliced

Instructions:

1. Prepare the Tofu Larb:
   - Heat vegetable oil in a skillet over medium-high heat. Add shallots, garlic, Thai chilies, and chopped lemongrass. Sauté until fragrant, about 2-3 minutes.
   - Add the crumbled tofu to the skillet. Cook until the tofu is lightly browned and heated through, about 5-7 minutes.
   - Stir in fish sauce, lime juice, soy sauce, and erythritol or monk fruit sweetener (if using). Cook for an additional 2-3 minutes.
   - Remove from heat and let cool slightly.
2. Prepare the Salad Ingredients:

- In a large mixing bowl, combine the mixed salad greens, thinly sliced cucumber, julienned or grated carrot, chopped cilantro, chopped mint, and sliced green onions.
3. Assemble the Salad:
   - Add the cooked tofu larb to the salad mixture in the large mixing bowl. Toss gently to combine.
4. Serve:
   - Divide the Low-carb Thai Tofu Larb Salad with Lemongrass among serving plates.

Enjoy this Low-carb Thai Tofu Larb Salad with Lemongrass as a light and flavorful meal. The combination of seasoned tofu infused with lemongrass and fresh salad greens is sure to tantalize your taste buds!

Thai-inspired Egg Salad with Chili Lime Dressing

Ingredients:

For the Salad:

- 6 hard-boiled eggs, peeled and chopped
- 1/2 cup cherry tomatoes, halved
- 1/4 cup red onion, thinly sliced
- 1/4 cup cucumber, diced
- 2 tablespoons chopped fresh cilantro
- 2 tablespoons chopped fresh mint
- 2 green onions, thinly sliced
- Salt and pepper to taste

For the Chili Lime Dressing:

- 2 tablespoons lime juice
- 1 tablespoon fish sauce
- 1 tablespoon soy sauce or tamari (for gluten-free option)
- 1 tablespoon honey or maple syrup
- 1 teaspoon grated ginger
- 1 clove garlic, minced
- 1 Thai bird's eye chili, finely chopped (adjust to taste)
- 1 tablespoon vegetable oil

Instructions:

1. Prepare the Salad:
   - In a large mixing bowl, combine the chopped hard-boiled eggs, halved cherry tomatoes, thinly sliced red onion, diced cucumber, chopped cilantro, chopped mint, and sliced green onions. Season with salt and pepper to taste.
2. Make the Chili Lime Dressing:
   - In a small bowl, whisk together lime juice, fish sauce, soy sauce or tamari, honey or maple syrup, grated ginger, minced garlic, and finely chopped Thai bird's eye chili. Slowly whisk in the vegetable oil until well combined.
3. Assemble the Salad:

- Pour the chili lime dressing over the salad ingredients in the large mixing bowl. Toss gently until everything is evenly coated with the dressing.
4. Serve:
   - Divide the Thai-inspired Egg Salad with Chili Lime Dressing among serving plates.
   - Optionally, garnish with additional cilantro and mint leaves.
   - Serve immediately and enjoy!

This Thai-inspired Egg Salad with Chili Lime Dressing offers a burst of flavors with every bite, making it a delightful and refreshing dish for any occasion!

Low-carb Thai Beef Salad with Bean Sprouts

Ingredients:

For the Beef:

- 1 lb (450g) beef steak (such as sirloin or flank), thinly sliced
- 2 tablespoons vegetable oil
- Salt and pepper to taste

For the Salad:

- 4 cups bean sprouts
- 1 cucumber, julienned
- 1 red bell pepper, thinly sliced
- 1 yellow bell pepper, thinly sliced
- 1/4 cup chopped fresh cilantro
- 1/4 cup chopped fresh mint
- 2 green onions, thinly sliced

For the Dressing:

- 3 tablespoons lime juice
- 2 tablespoons fish sauce
- 1 tablespoon soy sauce or tamari (for gluten-free option)
- 1 tablespoon sesame oil
- 1 tablespoon erythritol or monk fruit sweetener (optional)
- 1 teaspoon grated ginger
- 1 clove garlic, minced
- 1 Thai bird's eye chili, finely chopped (adjust to taste)

Instructions:

1. Prepare the Beef:
    - Heat vegetable oil in a skillet over medium-high heat. Season the thinly sliced beef with salt and pepper.
    - Cook the beef in the skillet for 2-3 minutes per side, or until cooked to your desired doneness. Remove from heat and let it rest for a few minutes. Slice thinly against the grain.
2. Prepare the Salad:

- In a large mixing bowl, combine the bean sprouts, julienned cucumber, thinly sliced red and yellow bell peppers, chopped cilantro, chopped mint, and sliced green onions.

3. Make the Dressing:
   - In a small bowl, whisk together lime juice, fish sauce, soy sauce or tamari, sesame oil, erythritol or monk fruit sweetener (if using), grated ginger, minced garlic, and finely chopped Thai bird's eye chili.

4. Assemble the Salad:
   - Add the sliced beef to the salad mixture in the large mixing bowl.

5. Toss with Dressing:
   - Pour the dressing over the salad ingredients. Toss gently until everything is evenly coated with the dressing.

6. Serve:
   - Divide the Low-carb Thai Beef Salad with Bean Sprouts among serving plates.
   - Optionally, garnish with additional chopped cilantro and mint leaves.
   - Serve immediately and enjoy!

This Low-carb Thai Beef Salad with Bean Sprouts is light, flavorful, and packed with protein and veggies, making it a perfect option for a healthy and satisfying meal.

Thai-style Spicy Pork Larb Lettuce Wraps

Ingredients:

For the Pork Larb:

- 1 lb (450g) ground pork
- 2 tablespoons vegetable oil
- 3 shallots, finely chopped
- 3 cloves garlic, minced
- 1-2 Thai bird's eye chilies, finely chopped (adjust to taste)
- 2 tablespoons fish sauce
- 2 tablespoons lime juice
- 1 tablespoon soy sauce or tamari (for gluten-free option)
- 1 teaspoon erythritol or monk fruit sweetener (optional)
- Salt and pepper to taste

For Serving:

- Large lettuce leaves (such as butter or iceberg lettuce)
- Thinly sliced cucumber
- Thinly sliced red onion
- Chopped fresh cilantro
- Chopped fresh mint
- Lime wedges
- Crushed roasted peanuts (optional)

Instructions:

1. Cook the Pork Larb:
   - Heat vegetable oil in a skillet over medium-high heat. Add shallots, garlic, and Thai chilies. Sauté until fragrant, about 1-2 minutes.
   - Add the ground pork to the skillet. Cook until the pork is browned and cooked through, breaking it up with a spoon, about 5-7 minutes.
   - Stir in fish sauce, lime juice, soy sauce, and erythritol or monk fruit sweetener (if using). Cook for an additional 2-3 minutes.
   - Remove from heat and let cool slightly.
2. Prepare the Serving Ingredients:
   - Wash and dry the lettuce leaves. Arrange them on a serving platter.

- Prepare the thinly sliced cucumber, red onion, chopped cilantro, chopped mint, lime wedges, and crushed peanuts (if using).
3. Assemble the Lettuce Wraps:
   - Spoon the cooked pork larb onto each lettuce leaf.
   - Top with thinly sliced cucumber, red onion, chopped cilantro, and chopped mint.
4. Serve:
   - Garnish the Thai-style Spicy Pork Larb Lettuce Wraps with lime wedges and crushed peanuts (if using).
   - Serve immediately and enjoy!

These Thai-style Spicy Pork Larb Lettuce Wraps are perfect as a light and flavorful appetizer or as a main course. They're packed with savory, spicy flavors and the freshness of the lettuce and herbs.

www.ingramcontent.com/pod-product-compliance
Lightning Source LLC
LaVergne TN
LVHW081806130125
800879LV00020B/841